The Principalship from A to Z

Ronald Williamson
Barbara R. Blackburn

EYE ON EDUCATION
6 DEPOT WAY WEST, SUITE 106
LARCHMONT, NY 10538
(914) 833–0551
(914) 833–0761 fax
www.eyeoneducation.com

Library of Congress Cataloging-in-Publication Data

Williamson, Ronald

The principalship from A to Z / Ronald Williamson, Barbara R. Blackburn.

    p. cm.

  ISBN 978-1-59667-105-8

1. School principals. 2. School management and organization. I. blackburn, Barbara R., 1961 - II. title.

LB2831.9.W55 2008

371.2'012--dc22

2008043904

1 0 9 8 7 6 5 4 3 2

Also Available from EYE ON EDUCATION

Rigor Is Not a Four-Letter Word
Barbara R. Blackburn

Classroom Motivation from A to Z:
How to Engage Your Students in Learning
Barbara R. Blackburn

Study Guide to Above
Barbara R. Blackburn

Classroom Instruction from A to Z:
How to Promote Student Learning
Barbara R. Blackburn

Study Guide to Above
Barbara R. Blackburn

Literacy from A to Z:
Engaging Students in Reading, Writing, Speaking, & Listening
Barbara R. Blackburn

Study Guide to Above
Barbara R. Blackburn

Get Organized!
Time Management for School Leaders
Frank Buck

What Great Principals Do *Differently*:
15 Things That Matter Most
Todd Whitaker

Motivating and Inspiring Teachers, 2nd Edition:
The Educational Leaders' Guide for Building Staff Morale
Todd Whitaker, Beth Whitaker, and Dale Lumpa

Improving Your School One Week at a Time
Jeffrey Zoul

Managing Conflict:
50 Strategies for School Leaders
Stacey Edmonson, Julie Combs, and Sandra Harris

Dedication

I dedicate this book to my wife Marsha, my partner for more than 40 years. You continually amaze me with your capacity for unconditional love, support, patience, and understanding. I am a better person because of my life with you.

—Ronald Williamson

I dedicate this book to the three principals who have influenced me in lasting ways. To Gene Gallelli, who hired me as a brand-new teacher and believed in me through my stumbles; to Ron Wilson, who provided me with multiple opportunities to grow as a teacher-leader; and to Bob Heath, whose partnership through our Professional Development School taught me the importance of inspiring teachers.

—Barbara R. Blackburn

Acknowledgments

We would like to thank the following people who supported our work:

- Our families and friends for their encouragement
- Bob Sickles for his confidence in our work
- Howard and Lucinda Johnston for their contributions to the chapter on effective school and classroom discipline
- Frank Buck for his contributions to Chapter J: Juggling Priorities and our list of principal resources
- Robert Blackburn for his expertise and assistance in Chapter K: Keys to Successful Public Relations
- Dirk Adkinson, an elementary principal in the Mukilteo School District outside Seattle, for reading, critiquing, and clarifying our thinking about the "real" work of a school principal
- Those thoughtful reviewers who read early drafts of this manuscript: Michael C. Alessandroni, Joseph Brown, Lee Ann Dumas, Eve Ford, Chuck Fradley, Sherryl Houdek, Don Kachur, and Andrew Paciulli.
- Colleagues in the Department of Leadership and Counseling at Eastern Michigan University and the Department of Curriculum and Instruction at Winthrop University, who are a continual source of support and positive reinforcement

The hundreds of principals we have worked with in every part of the nation—you hold one of the most demanding jobs in the world, but you, along with your teachers, are the greatest hope for improving the educational experience of all students

Meet the Authors

Ronald Williamson is a professor of leadership and counseling at Eastern Michigan University. Previously, he taught at the University of North Carolina and was a teacher, principal, and executive director of instruction in the Ann Arbor, Michigan, Public Schools.

Ron also served as executive director of the National Middle School Association, a as member of Middle Level Council of the National Association of Secondary School Principals (NASSP), and as president of the National Forum to Accelerate Middle Grades Reform. He received the Gruhn- Long-Melton Award from NASSP in recognition of lifetime achievement in secondary school leadership, the Teaching Excellence Award from the University of North Carolina at Greensboro, and the Alumni Teaching Excellence Award from Eastern Michigan University.

The author of more than 100 books, chapters, papers, and articles in all the major professional journals serving middle and high school teachers and administrators, Ron works with schools throughout the country on issues of school improvement.

Ron provided direct services to several large urban school districts when he was selected by the Edna McConnell Clark Foundation to act as a leadership coach in its national school reform project. He also worked with the Galef Institute in Los Angeles on a Comprehensive School Reform project to improve schools in New York City, Houston, Louisville, and Los Angeles. Currently, he is serving as an assessment and scheduling consultant as well as editor of research briefs for the Principals' Partnership, a program of the Union Pacific Foundation.

Barbara R. Blackburn has taught early childhood, elementary, middle, and high school students and has served as an educational consultant for three publishing companies. She holds a master's degree in is school administration and is certified as a school principal in North Carolina. She received her doctorate in curriculum and instruction from the University of North Carolina at Greensboro. In 2006, she earned the Outstanding Junior Professor Award at Winthrop University. Now an assistant professor at the University of North Carolina at Charlotte, she teaches graduate courses and collaborates with area schools on special projects.

In addition to speaking at state and national conferences, she also presents workshops for teachers and administrators in elementary, middle, and high schools. Her most popular workshops include the following:

Instructional Strategies That Motivate Students

Content Literacy Strategies for the Young and the Restless

Motivation and Assessment

Rigor Is NOT a Four Letter Word

Motivating Yourself and Others

Engaging Instruction Leads to Higher Achievement

High Expectations and Increased Support Lead to Success

If you'd like information about inviting Barbara Blackburn to speak to your group, please contact her at her Web site: www.barbarablackburnonline.com. We also invite you to send us your feedback as you implement the ideas from the book.

Table of Contents

Topical Index

Correlations to the ISLLC and ELCC Standards are
included in the Appendices that begin on page 209.

Free Downloads

Many of the charts and templates displayed in this book can be downloaded and printed out by anyone who has purchased this book. Book buyers have permission to download and print out these Adobe Acrobat documents.

You can access these downloads by visiting Eye On Education's Web site: www.eyeoneducation.com. Click on FREE Downloads. Or search or browse our Web site from our homepage to find this book and then scroll down for downloading instructions.

You'll need your book-buyer access code: **PRI-7105-8**

Index of Downloads

Introduction

We believe in the power of principals, working collaboratively with their teachers, to make a difference in the lives of students every day. We recognize, however, the complexity of the job, the need to balance competing priorities, and the high-stakes environment in which you work.

In light of this, we decided to write a book that would provide principals with a set of tools that can be immediately used to improve their practice. It is not lock-step program, nor is it a checklist. It does provide a set of recommended activities that, when consistently and persistently applied, will help you be more effective.

The Principalship from A to Z is organized into 26 chapters, one for each letter of the alphabet. The chapters are not sequential; they are organized around topics and areas of interest. You may start with any area that interests you or meets a current need. It may be helpful to look at the Topical Index on page 15 first to get an overview of the entire book. On page 210, you will find the Interstate School Leaders Licensure Consortium (ISLLC) Standards correlated to the chapters. There is also a correlation to the Educational Leadership Constituent Council (ELCC) Standards on page 215.

Our focus in this book is simple: to provide a practical guide with specific strategies that will help you navigate the many tasks you face as a principal. Each chapter is organized in a consistent manner. You will begin with "Think About It," a short question to prompt your thinking about a specific area of responsibility. Throughout the chapter, you will find are easy-to-read charts that summarize or extend the examples we discuss, as well as samples of recommended ideas, such as walk-through templates or mission statements. Each chapter concludes with a summary of "Skills for Principals" related to the topic. Because each chapter is a synopsis of information, you may want more detail on certain topics. After the Skills for Principals section, you will find a list of recommended resources.

We believe that the greatest opportunity for a student's future success lies in the hands of principals and their teachers. We hope the strategies suggested in this book help you as you face that challenge.

A

Achievement Is the Focus

For to change the norms, the very foci of attention, of a cultural system is a difficult task—far more complex than that of changing an individual's attitudes and interests.

James S. Coleman

Think About It

Is student achievement the main focus in your school? How is that evidenced?

As a principal, you are pulled in a variety of directions on any given day. You are expected to manage personnel, handle discipline issues, improve instruction, and maintain student safety, all while following relevant case law. That is just the starting point; the list of responsibilities can seem overwhelming. Throughout this book, we'll look at each of the core responsibilities of a principal.

However, it's important to begin with the most important role. We believe that student learning is the primary role of schools. It's not just one of the roles of schools; it is the most important role. Despite competing demands, the most successful principals are those who recognize this importance and align every school activity with the school's achievement agenda.

In this chapter, we'll look at how to make decisions using a lens of student achievement, the principal's role in an achievement-oriented school, and how to measure achievement.

Making Decisions Through a Lens of Achievement

Effective principals adopt a "whatever it takes" stance toward student achievement. Every school activity is seen through the lens of student learning. Consider this question: "How would _____ positively impact student learning?" A principal gave it to us when we explained that most high-performing schools make decisions based on the answer to that question. Making decisions through a lens of student achievement means that we filter our choices through this question, choosing the answer that has the most positive impact on student learning.

Sample Questions

How does our schedule give priority to student learning?

Do we have a range of student activities that support our school's mission?

How do we incorporate a range of instructional practices into each lesson?

How do we use data on student learning to guide decisions about program design?

How does this activity support our school's academic mission?

The Principal's Role in an Achievement-Oriented School

Ultimately, your role in an achievement-oriented school is threefold. You must be an instructional leader, a human resource developer, and a change agent to truly spotlight achievement. We'll give a short overview of these roles, but you will also find information related to specific activities in the remainder of the book.

Instructional Leader with Inspiration

In order to move your school toward an achievement focus, you will need to understand the academic mission of the school and use every opportunity to talk about that mission with students, staff, families, and community (see Chapter B: Beginnings, Endings, and School Culture). Effective principals talk about achievement with staff and parents at parent–teacher organization meetings, community and church activities, neighborhood gatherings, and board of education meetings.

Improving the instructional program for students is the highest priority. Regularly meet with individuals and groups of faculty to discuss the achievement of their students and to develop plans for improving student achievement. Make improved student learning central to all discussions with staff (see Chapter I: It's All About Instruction and Chapter Q: Quality Teacher Evaluation).

Next, actively engage students, staff, and the community in school governance, particularly the review of achievement data and the development of plans to improve student learning (see Chapter F: Focusing on Data). As you work with staff and the community to gather, analyze, and report achievement data, recognize staff members for academic achievement and use recognition to maintain high standards for all students.

Sample Ways to Focus on Achievement

Create posters with a catchphrase such as "Learning is not optional."

Be sure that achievement is part of your school mission.

Talk about student learning and achievement at all meetings.

Use staff meetings as a time to focus on instructional improvement.

Make a banner displaying the school's achievement slogan and hang it in the lobby.

Recognize teachers and students who make a difference in the school's achievement agenda.

Discuss achievement in every school newsletter.

Make achievement discussions a routine part of school life by including the topic in parent conferences, staff meetings, and in school newsletters. Broaden your influence outside the school building by establishing liaisons with families and community agencies to ensure that students' physical and socio-emotional health is maintained and that students have support and encouragement for the school's academic mission (see Chapter T: Teaming with Families and Communities). Throughout all of these activities, model the use of appropriate interpersonal and instructional strategies to set a vision for the future.

Principal as Human Resource Developer

Your second role is that of a developer of human resources. In this area, understand that students have a variety of learning styles and a range of development needs. Work with teachers to ensure that all students are challenged with appropriately high expectations and that the instructional program provides for the diverse learning styles of all students (see Chapter I: It's All About Instruction).

Similarly, establish high expectations for staff performance. This includes participating in professional development, using a variety of instructional strategies, providing support to students who engage in academically challenging experiences, monitoring student learning, and adjusting teaching practices to ensure high levels of student performance. As a part of each performance evaluation, discuss how faculty members use innovative practices and the levels of instructional and curricular effectiveness (see Chapters P, Q, S, and W).

Support faculty as they try new instructional and curricular practices and understand that a lack of success with those practices is an opportunity to learn, refine, and strengthen instructional skills. Provide professional development activities that focus on improving curricular and instructional practice (see Chapter P: Professional Development). Work with staff members to develop and maintain a curricular program that provides rigor and challenge for all students. Rigorous scientific thought, the arts, foreign language, mathematical reasoning, and written and oral expression should be an integral part of the program for all students, not simply those in honors courses or on a college-bound track (see Chapter I: It's All About Instruction).

Principal as Change Agent

Embedded within the first two roles is the job of being a change agent. Recognize and act on the knowledge that students learn at different rates, have varied interests, and come to school with a variety of experiences and backgrounds. Build accountability for student achievement into every aspect of the school's program. Take responsibility for student learning, use data as a basis for instructional decision making, and take every opportunity to address achievement issues (see Chapter F).

Work with teachers to create organizational structures that ensure every student is known by at least one adult and that each student's achievement is closely monitored. Provide for the effective use of school time, avoid interruptions to the instructional program, and ensure productive and purposeful classroom activities (see Chapter M: Managing Schedules). Attend to the academic needs of all students regardless of previous school experience by providing all students with a rigorous intellectual experience that requires the use of learning rather than storage and retrieval.

Establish and support a co-curricular program that provides activities focused on academic and intellectual interests, as well as physical activity. Finally, employ a variety of achievement measures, including both standardized tests and district and classroom assessments, use of student products and demonstrations, and other measures of achievement.

Measuring Achievement

If student achievement is our goal, how do we measure it? First, it is important to become comfortable looking at and using data to guide discussions with staff and parents. Make a decision that you will view your data and use those data as you talk with your staff, parents, and students. In Chapter F: Focusing on Data, you will find specific suggestions for working with data.

Next, remember to use multiple measures. If you focus only on data from standardized tests, you are limiting the conversation. We strongly believe that standardized test scores should be your starting point, not the finish line. Be sure to look at a wide range of formal and informal data.

Possible Data Sources

- Standardized achievement tests
- Local assessments
- Diagnostic tests
- Student portfolios/projects
- Teacher grades
- Dropout rates
- Student demographics
- Teacher demographics (experience, professional development)

Third, use the data as a part of your discussions with teachers, parents, older students, and other stakeholders. One principal commented, "Our test scores aren't great. So I just don't talk about them." That does a disservice to your faculty and students. It's important to share information about test scores and other data. Use the scores as a stepping stone to discuss what is going on in your school. Share the positive focus, growth points, and goals for the futures. If you simply ignore your data, you are allowing others to define you simply by the numbers.

Questions to Guide the Conversation

- What is the status of the achievement agenda in our school?
- How does the achievement of our students compare with the achievement of schools in our district/county?
- What is the distribution of achievement among students based on gender, ethnicity, or socioeconomic status?
- What is the perception of achievement in our school among students, parents, faculty, and the community?
- What specific activities take place in our school to promote conversations and discussion of achievement?
- What professional development is provided at our school to ensure improved student achievement?
- What groups or individuals are participating in development of an Achievement Improvement Plan?
- Who is accountable for improved achievement in our school?
- What is the achievement "bottom line" in our school?

A Final Note

The job of a principal is multifaceted and complex. In the following chapters, we'll be providing a summary of key aspects of your job. However, each of these should be viewed through one lens: The primary role of the school is to help students learn.

Skills for Principals

- Develop a shared vision of high performance for every student.
- Mobilize staff to achieve the school's vision.
- Work to develop a coherent and rigorous curriculum.
- Create a personalized, motivating, and engaging learning environment for every student.
- Provide appropriate instructional supervision.
- Develop the instructional capacity of teachers and other staff.
- Utilize assessment and accountability systems to monitor student progress.

If You Would Like More Information . . .

Authentic Achievement: Restructuring Schools for Intellectual Quality, edited by Fred M. Newmann (Jossey-Bass, 1996)

Building Background Knowledge for Academic Achievement: Research on What Works in Schools, by Robert J. Marzano (Association for Supervision and Curriculum Development, 2004)

Improving Achievement in Low-Performing Schools: Key Results for School Leaders, by Randolph E. Ward and Mary Ann Burke (Corwin, 2004)

Education Trust—information on school reform focused on closing the achievement gap among students: http://www.edtrust.org

Closing the Achievement Gap Resources—an ERIC report on strategies for addressing the achievement gap: http://www.eric digests.org/2002-3/gap.htm

Organizing Time, Space, Staff, and Resources to Improve Student Achievement—helpful suggestions from the Southern Regional Education Board: http://www.sreb.org/main/Leadership/Modules/descriptions/Organizing.pdf

B

Beginnings, Endings, and School Culture

The heart and soul of school culture is what people believe, the assumptions they make about how school works.

Thomas Sergiovanni

Think About It

What is the perception of the culture at your school? Does everyone (teachers, administrators, parents, students) perceive it in the same way?

How would you define school culture? It's a rather vague concept, isn't it? Some talk about culture as the overall feeling about a school or the perception of the school, but that is really more the climate of a school.

Climate or Culture

School climate and school culture are distinct. The climate of a school reflects the "feeling or tone" of the school, the relationships among personnel, and the morale of the setting.

Culture reflects a more complex set of values, traditions, and patterns of behavior that are present in a school. The culture is indicative of deeply embedded beliefs about schooling. Culture reveals itself in "the unwritten rules and assumptions, the combination of rituals and traditions, the array of symbols and artifacts, the special language and phrasing that staff and students use, the expectations for change and learning" (Peterson & Deal, 2002).

Culture reflects the unspoken norms about school operations and is transmitted from generation to generation, often by the influential staff whom others recognize as informal leaders and opinion leaders. As we consider school culture and your role in influencing that culture, Bolman and Deal (2003) provide a model for understanding the factors that contribute to culture. It is based on the idea that organizations are cultures and reflect underlying values, which are patterns of shared basic assumptions. These assumptions are often taught to new members of the culture—whether teachers, students, or parents—as the "correct" way to act, think, perceive, and feel.

Principals can impact the school culture by using these symbols to promote institutional values and the school's core mission. Most importantly, principals need to understand the power of these symbols to telegraph messages about what is important.

Organizational Symbols That Reflect Culture

- Rituals and ceremonies provide structure to our daily life and to the routine of a school. Rituals occur routinely, whereas ceremonies are grander, less frequent events (graduation). Both rituals and ceremonies reflect values in their structure and priority, and they carry meaning about what is valued and what is important.

- Heroes and heroines are those people whom we look up to as reflecting the organization's values—people who are examples of living those values.

- Stories and tales are recollections of events that are told and retold and play a powerful role in sharing examples of organizational values. Stories often contain a moral and are inevitably engaging.

- Rewards and reinforcements reflect those things that are valued and therefore rewarded. Is it creativity in the classroom or compliance with established patterns? Is it waiving a rule so that a student may be successful or adhering to established policy?

How is each of these evidenced in your school? Who are the heroes and heroines? What are the important stories that are told to newcomers? What is the reward system—both formal and informal?

Cultural Factors	Examples
Rituals and ceremonies	Attendance procedures Graduation Welcoming activities for new students
Heroes and heroines	Student recognition Teacher recognition systems
Stories and tales	Informal descriptions of school activities Recollection of memorable school events or people shared with others
Reward system	Evaluation procedures Allocation of professional development resources

Although each of these is an important area that influences school culture, we'll spend the remaining part of the chapter dealing with one: rituals and ceremonies.

Critical Rituals: Beginning and Ending the Year

Among the most important rituals in a school are the ways in which the year begins and ends. Successful principals recognize the power of rituals to shape school culture.

Beginnings Set the Tone

The start of a school year is an ideal time to shape or reinforce the culture of your school. For most stakeholders, the new year is exciting. It is filled with both the promise of a new beginning and the nervous anticipation of that start. Your job is twofold: to help everyone feel safe and secure as they antic- ipate the year, and to set a tone that reflects your vision for the future. At the beginning of every school year at one Michigan high school, for example, faculty, staff, and tenth-, eleventh-, and twelfth-grade students lined the hallway and clapped as incoming ninth-graders entered the building for the first time. Another school posted the name and picture of every new student in the main entrance to the school.

Activities Prior to the Opening of School

- Send a welcome letter to staff with information about assignment, rooms, student rosters (if possible).
- Permit teachers to get into their rooms and prepare for the opening of school.
- Distribute supplies to teacher rooms.
- Plan for opening day activities.
- Provide a time for parents and students to visit the school, particularly new families.
- If you have a number of parents who speak a language other than English, prepare school registration and information materials in their native language (most often Spanish).

It's also important to celebrate the first day of school. You might identify a theme and then use that throughout the school year to keep everyone focused. A Michigan principal used *Results* (1999) as the theme one year. Every teacher received a copy of *Results Now* by Mike Schmoker (2006) and was invited to read it over the summer.

Opening Day Activities for Staff

- Recognize that teachers want to work in their rooms and prepare for the arrival of students.
- Ensure that opening day is upbeat and positive.
- Provide food.
- Model good instructional practices.
- Rather than scheduling additional meetings, use an alternative means for making announcements (e-mail, newsletter).
- Use upbeat and positive stories to set the tone for the year. A principal in Tempe, Arizona, used "Turn Around" stories to provide examples of students who had made significant changes in their academic performance. The school had a history of low achievement, and staff were concerned that it was difficult to make achievement gains with students.

Of course, don't forget to plan opening day activities for parents and students. Be sure that lots of helpful adults are available to assist students and their families in locating classrooms, lockers, and so on. Have plenty of directional signs, clearly posted in the languages of your student population. Be sure that every student is scheduled and assigned to a teacher; one of the worst nightmares for a student and parent is to sit in the office on the first day of school, knowing they don't really "belong." Finally, encourage your staff to smile. For anyone walking in the door, it makes a difference to feel welcome!

Endings Leave a Mark

The end of the school year provides an opportunity to celebrate success and to lay the groundwork for the next school year. A principal in South Carolina told us, "No matter how tired we are, we take time to celebrate the year and look forward to the next year." Ultimately, people remember how something ended, so use that time to your advantage.

Remember to identify and celebrate academic and social successes and share them with staff and parents. This builds confidence that the work of teachers and parents makes a difference. A high school principal in Tacoma, Washington, took photos of classroom and student activities throughout the year. The school's Photography Club turned the photos into a collection of posters that were placed in the lobby, the cafeteria, and the hallways of the school to celebrate the year. The principal remarked, "Students like these photos. They spend lots of time looking at them and recalling the year. Rather than acting out it ends the year on a much more positive tone."

Prior to the end of the year, review data about the current year (achievement data, climate data, satisfaction data) with the School Improvement Team and identify goals and strategies for the coming year. Based on this plan, identify a theme for the coming year. The school in Michigan adopted a second-year theme of "Even Greater Results" that built on the prior theme of "Results." Be sure to schedule a time and/or means to share with families the success of the year and discuss the goals for the coming year. This helps build their continued ownership. Finally, arrange an end-of-the-year activity with staff to celebrate successes. One school in Ohio, for example, always had a faculty potluck at lunchtime on the last day, as it is an early-release day for students. It provides a time to socialize, build camaraderie, and celebrate.

A Final Note

The culture of your school is a reflection of the beliefs of those who work and visit. Planning rituals and ceremonies can be time-consuming, but the results are worth it. School culture affects all facets of your work. Invest in it.

Skills for Principals

- Nurture and sustain a trusting, collaborative work environment.
- Recognize the powerful role of school practices to shape school culture.
- Understand the importance of symbolic activities at the beginning and end of the school year to convey the school's values.
- Plan opening and closing activities that provide time to reflect on and celebrate the school's accomplishments.

If You Would Like More Information . . .

The Shaping School Culture Fieldbook, by Kent D. Peterson and Terrence E. Deal (Jossey-Bass, 2002)

Shaping School Culture: The Heart of Leadership, by Terrence E. Deal and Kent D. Peterson (Jossey-Bass, 1999)

Building an Intentional School Culture: Excellence in Academics and Character, by Charles F. Elbot and David Vance Fulton (Corwin, 2008)

"Leading Edge: Culture Shift Doesn't Occur Overnight—or Without Conflict," by Rick DuFour, *Journal of Staff Development,* Fall 2004: http://www.nsdc.org/library/publications/jsd/dufour254.cfm

Center for Improving School Culture: http://www.schoolculture.net

"Leadership for an Improved School Culture: How to Assess and Improve the Culture of Your School," by Dr. Christopher Wagner, Kentucky School Leader: http://www.schoolculture.net/ky schoolleaderfall04.pdf

"The Principal's Role in Shaping School Culture," by E. Redalen: http://resources.sai-iowa.org/culture/index.html

C

Conducting Successful Meetings

As teamwork and cross-organizational projects increase, meetings become the setting in which much of the really important work gets done. Now more than ever team and organizational success is reliant on the quality of its meetings.

From *Death by Meeting*, by Peter Lencioni

Think About It

How much of your time is spent in meetings? How often are you in charge of a meeting?

If you are like most of the principals we work with, you spend more time than you would like in meetings. And you've likely spent much time that you considered unproductive. When you are conducting a meeting, you want participants to feel that it was a successful, productive meeting. If that is your goal, remember this: Successful meetings are thoughtfully planned and implemented. As you plan, there are four questions to consider.

Planning Questions

What is the purpose of the meeting?

What is being decided?

Who decides?

What are the meeting standards and norms?

What Is the Purpose of the Meeting?

You may be thinking, "Of course I need to plan a purpose. Who doesn't do that?" But we've been to far too many meetings where the purpose was unclear, unstated, or unknown. Think about it this way: Are you conducting a meeting in order to discuss and identify options and alternatives for a situation, or is the end result to make a decision? If you want to bring together a group of stakeholders to gather input, that is appropriate, but if they believe they are meeting to make a decision, then your meeting begins with a conflict, and it is less likely to be productive.

What Is Being Decided?

Next, turn your attention to the specific agenda. It's important for participants to have a clear idea of what is to be discussed. The agenda may be developed collaboratively, but plan for that in advance. An agenda can also help you budget your time appropriately, so all information is covered. As you plan, ask yourself, "By the end of the meeting, will participants have the information they need to make a decision on the issue?" You might also consider whether your agenda allows for adequate discussion to inform the decision.

Characteristics of Quality Agendas

- Clearly state the purpose and/or goals of the meeting.
- Review agreed-upon operational norms and norms of collaboration.
- Provide clarity about the action to be taken (e.g., discussion, decision).
- Indicate the time allotted for each item.
- Provide time for reflection and processing of information.
- Include time at the end of the meeting to clarify what information should be shared and by whom.

Who Decides?

Prior to the meeting, determine the role of the group in terms of decision making. Is the task of the group to make a decision? Perhaps it is to make a recommendation or to study the issue. Is the decision-making body clear? For example, will the decision be made by the principal alone or by the principal with input? Perhaps the goal is for the decision to be made by the administrator with staff consensus or by the staff with administrative input. Or the decision may be made by the staff by consensus or by the staff by a majority vote. You may even have a subgroup making the decision. Each of these strategies is appropriate for certain situations; however, everyone needs to clearly understand their role.

Several years ago, while waiting to present a staff development session to elementary school teachers, we observed a principal conducting a short meeting. He explained that a decision needed to be made regarding staffing and personnel responsibilities for the next school year, and that it would be decided based on a vote from teachers and other staff. Everyone voted on a ballot, and at lunch, the principal privately explained that he was disappointed in the results. He said that he had trusted the staff to make the right decision, and they didn't. Then he said, "I'm going to tell them that we aren't doing it that way, we are going to do it my way." The morale of the teachers and staff plummeted, and the principal lost all credibility. That's exactly the situation you want to avoid.

As you determine who will make the decision, also consider the timeline for the decision, and make that clear to participants. Finally, determine how the decision will be shared with or communicated to the larger school community.

Planning Guide for Decision Making

Primary Decision Maker	Secondary Decision Makers	Stakeholders to Provide Input

What Are the Meeting Standards and Norms?

A crucial part of any effective meeting is having a set of meeting standards or operational norms. This includes basic decisions such as the seating arrangements. If you want an open discussion, try to arrange for participants to face each other, perhaps around a table or in a semicircle rather than in rows. Set a firm start and end time, and stick to them. This shows that you respect the participants' time. If the meeting is lengthy, plan for a break, but again, set a time and adhere to that. Be sure that any speaker knows his or her allocated time and stays within those parameters.

Ask yourself, "How will we maintain our group memory of discussion and decisions?" Do you want to use charts posted visibly in the room, or will you have someone record notes? In today's age of technology, how can you utilize the equipment you have to support the process? You might even consider recording the meeting. A public recording provides visual clues, develops shared ownership, minimizes repetition, reduces status differences among participants, and makes accountability easier.

What are the guidelines for discussion? We often use a "parking lot," which is simply a poster in the room. Participants are given sticky notes, and if there is a question or discussion item that is off the topic, they write it on a note and post it in the parking lot. You can revisit those items at the end of the meeting if there is time, or you can discuss them individually or at another time.

It's also important to model collaborative discussion. Allowing adequate wait time in response to questions, asking open-ended questions, and giving everyone a chance to speak are the foundational elements of a collaborative discussion. Garmston and Wellman (1999) describe seven norms of collaboration that are helpful as you facilitate discussions.

Seven Norms of Collaboration

- **Pausing**: Pausing before responding or asking a question allows time for thinking and enhances dialogue, discussion and decision making.

- **Paraphrasing**: Using a paraphrase starter that is comfortable for you, such as "As you are . . ." or "You're thinking . . . ," and following the starter with a paraphrase assists members of the group to hear and understand each other as they formulate decisions.

- **Probing**: Using gentle open-ended probes or inquiries such as, "Please say more . . ." or "I'm curious about . . ." or "I'd like to hear more about . . ." or "Then, are you saying . . . ?" increases the clarity and precision of the group's thinking.

- **Putting ideas on the table**: Ideas are the heart of a meaningful dialogue. Label the intention of your comments. For example, you might say, "Here is one idea . . ." or "One thought I have is . . ." or "Here is a possible approach . . ."

- **Paying attention to self and others**: Meaningful dialogue is facilitated when each group member is conscious of self and of others and is aware of not only what he or she is saying but also how it is said and how others are responding. This includes paying attention to learning style when planning for, facilitating, and participating in group meetings.

- **Presuming positive intentions**: Assuming that others' intentions are positive promotes and facilitates meaningful dialogue and eliminates unintentional put-downs. Using positive intentions in your speech is one manifestation of this norm.

- **Pursuing a balance between advocacy and inquiry**: Pursuing and maintaining a balance between advocating a position and inquiring about one's own and others' positions assists the group to become a learning organization.

Source: Garmston & Wellman (1999).

A Final Note

Ultimately, good meetings are interactive and provide for balanced participation. As you plan, find ways to engage every participant in the discussion. In addition to building ownership in the process, your participants will be more productive, and your meetings will be a success.

Skills for Principals

Recognize the importance of and develop the capacity for distributed leadership.

Organize meetings so that they are productive and support the attainment of school goals.

Focus school activities to support a high-quality educational experience for students.

Acknowledge the valuable accomplishments of teachers and other staff.

Value the involvement of school constituents in decisions regarding school programs and school life.

If You Would Like More Information . . .

Meeting of the Minds: A Guide to Successful Meeting Facilitation, by Daniel S. Iacofano (MIG Communications, 2001)

Great Meetings! Great Results, by Dee Kelsey and Pam Plumb (Hanson Park Press, 2004)

Facilitate Don't Frustrate! A Collection of Practical and Proven Tips for Facilitating Team Meetings, by Deb McCormick (TEAMed UP, 2006)

General guidelines for conducting successful meetings: http://www.skagitwatershed.org/~donclark/leader/leadmet.html, http://www.managementhelp.org/misc/mtgmgmnt.htm

Information on the Seven Norms of Collaboration, available at the Adaptive Schools Web site: http://www.adaptiveschools.com

D

Data-Driven Decisions

While states have an important role to play in designing reliable data systems, ultimately, principals are responsible for making the best use of student data to improve teaching and learning in their school buildings.

Gerald Tirozzi,
executive director,
National Association of Secondary School Principals

Think About It

Are you overwhelmed with data? How do you use the data you have?

Many principals feel as if they are drowning in data, overwhelmed with the sheer amount of data they have, and unsure how to use the information. In this chapter, we'll look at a four-step approach to working with data.

Four-Step Approach

1. Determine what you want to know.

2. Decide how you will collect the data.

3. Analyze the data and results.

4. Set priorities and goals based on the analysis.

Determine What You Want to Know

First, determine what you want to know. Begin by looking at different kinds of data.

Types of Data

Demographic data: These data describe students and are most often used to understand student learning data. They provide insight into equity within your student learning data. Demographic data will reveal "who got it."

Achievement and learning data: These data tell us what is going on in a school or district. They tell us what students learned and what they achieved. These data help us understand how students are achieving. Student learning data will reveal "what students got."

Instructional process data: These are the data that help you understand why students achieved at the level they did. If student achievement in mathematics is low, you might look at the type of mathematics that students do, the time they spend on math, or the alignment of mathematics with state and local standards or benchmarks. School process data will reveal "how or why they got it." These data can include information about teacher participation in professional development.

Attitudinal data: These data tell you how people feel about a program and how they experience your school or district program. Attitudinal or perception data will reveal "how they feel or what they believe about it."

Select an area of focus and any demographic indicators. For example, do you want to determine whether your minority girls are performing lower in math? Then, write a set of data analysis questions.

Examples of Data Analysis Questions

- What is the distribution of student grades in mathematics based on gender and ethnicity?
- How do student scores on the state mathematics test compare when disaggregated by gender and ethnicity?
- What is the distribution of students based on gender and ethnicity in the different levels of mathematics?
- What academic support services are provided to minority female students?

Consider any factors that might narrow the questions and identify data sources and/or methods of data collection.

Collect Data

Next, collect data. You may need to simply locate readily available data or determine ways to gather local data about the focus area. Collected data should align with the data analysis questions. You might use a crosswalk (see below) to track the appropriate data to match each question.

Data Analysis Question	Demographic Data	Achievement andLearning Data	Tracking Processes Data	Attitudinal Data

You likely have data readily available to you. Examples include test score data, enrollment in classes, parent or student survey results, attendance patterns, and requests to drop/add classes and/or teachers.

If you need additional data, you might commission a study of local issues and concerns, provide time for teachers to shadow students, or design and administer a short survey. And don't forget that a powerful source of information is student work. You might conduct a walk-through with faculty to observe the school and student work or examine student work during grade-level, team, or department meetings (see Chapter L: Looking at Student Work and Chapter S: Seeing with New Eyes).

Other Ideas for Collecting Data

- Survey stakeholder groups (students, parents, teachers, administrators, counselors, support staff).
- Interview random members of each group concerning the program, philosophy, and climate.
- Conduct a shadow study of students.
- Assess specific components of the program (counseling services, reading, instructional strategies, curriculum).
- Gather currently available information (achievement tests, student grades, attendance).
- Conduct a self-study looking at alignment with published standards.
- Ask for an external review by a professional organization or a noted school researcher.
- Hold focus group interview with key stakeholder groups.
- Review pertinent information (department minutes, student schedules, student disciplinary referrals).

Analyze the Data and Results

As you begin to analyze your data, be sure to involve all constituents in the process.

Ways to Involve Constituents

- Ensure representative membership.
- Ensure participation by those with the most to lose or gain.
- Seek and involve "known dissenters."
- Have participants assist in the gathering and analysis of data and information.
- Seek members to contribute specific expertise to committee initiatives.
- Share newsletters and other communication vehicles with participants before distribution.
- Conduct the review as an open process so that those who are often excluded have every opportunity to participate.

Clarify specific tasks as well as the timeline so that everyone can participate appropriately. Planning thoughtfully and purposefully for the discussion is key to positive growth. One of the lessons we've learned about presenting and using data is the importance of presenting data in a nonthreatening way to ensure purposeful engagement. Finally, as you look in-depth at your data, discuss how you will share the results.

Set Priorities and Goals

Finally, work with your School Improvement Team or other collaborative group to determine priorities based on your area of focus and your data analysis.

Sample Priorities Based on Data Analysis

Midvale High School, Midvale, Michigan

The mission of the Midvale Area High School, above all else, is to educate each student to his or her greatest potential by establishing and maintaining high academic standards. It is only through the cooperative effort of students, parents, staff and community that this and the following can be achieved:

- Provide an academic and social transition from middle school to a more independent high school setting.
- Create and maintain a safe, caring, disciplined school environment.
- Enhance self-esteem through academic achievement and individual accomplishments.
- Promote an atmosphere where there is a sense of belonging, cooperation, personal responsibility and mutual respect.
- Prepare students for life-long learning and success (i.e., good citizenship, independent learning and life skills).

Once you have determined your priorities, goals, or area of focus, study and select strategies that will allow you to address the area of focus. This is a pivotal point. Too often, we gather and analyze data and set goals, but then we do not use that information to make decisions on an ongoing basis. We've developed five rules to guide you through the process.

Using Data to Set Priorities and Make Decisions

Rule #1: **Focus**—Select an area of focus and establish clear priorities. Too many improvement efforts falter because of a diffused focus.

Rule #2: **Be guided by questions**—Be clear about what you want to know and prepare data analysis questions to guide the collection of data and its analysis.

Rule #3: **Design thoughtful and provocative conversations**—Plan engaging discussions about the data. Raise provocative questions about those factors (classroom instructional) that contribute to understanding the data.

Rule #4: **Engage appropriate stakeholders**—It is vitally important that appropriate stakeholders contribute to the conversation and analysis of the data. Involvement builds support and capacity for school improvement.

Rule #5: **Focus**—Maintain the focus, select strategies aligned with the area of focus, and regularly monitor and adjust your improvement strategies.

A Final Note

Unfortunately, data are often simply stacks of numbers. However, if you dig deeper, invest in analytical discussions of the data, and use that information to help you plan, you can FOCUS and see your work pay off in results.

FOCUS

F	First things first.
O	Outline framework with questions.
C	Conversations planned for results.
U	Understand and engage all stakeholders.
S	Stay on track.

Skills for Principals

- Collect and analyze data and other information about the school's program.
- Ensure the evaluation of school programs.
- Use data to identify goals for improving the school's educational program for every student.
- Create a School Improvement Plan based on data about student learning, school climate, and instructional effectiveness;
- Monitor and adjust school improvement initiatives based on data.

If You Would Like More Information . . .

Results Now: How We Can Achieve Unprecedented Improvements in Teaching and Learning, by Mike Schmoker (Association for Supervision and Curriculum Development, 2006)

Using Data to Improve Student Learning, by Victoria L. Bernhardt (Eye On Education, 2003)

Data Analysis for Comprehensive Schoolwide Improvement, by Victoria L. Bernhardt (Eye On Education, 1998)

Using Data to Improve Student Achievement, by Deborah Wahlstrom (Successline, 1999)

A variety of resources of use of data are available from the Technology Alliance: http://www.3d2know.org/best_practices.html

A guidebook of ideas for using data: http://www.learningpt.org/pdfs/datause/guidebook.pdf

A variety of tools for use with data: http://www.annenberginstitute.org/tools/using_data/index.php

E

Effective School and Classroom Discipline

*Too many rules get in the way of leadership. They just put you in a box.
. . . People set rules to keep from making decisions.*

Coach Mike Krzyzewski

Think About It

How much of your time is taken up with discipline issues?

Dealing with discipline issues can be all-consuming for a principal. Therefore, it is important to understand the underlying causes of discipline problems and create a structure to minimize these problems.

First, we must recognize why students misbehave. Lucinda Johnston describes four main sources of misbehavior.

Sources of Misbehavior

Kids being kids: Normal kid exuberance coupled with a lack of sophistication or mature judgment.

Different agenda: Bored, unable to do class work, angry about something, or disturbed by events in their lives, students act out to draw attention to their needs.

Value incongruence: Because of experience, family circumstances or culture norms, student values may be incongruent with those of the school so that they are unable to act appropriately.

Disorders: Psychological and social disorders may range from very mild to extremely severe.

Policies and procedures should be appropriate for your school population, addressing the sources of misbehavior and taking into consideration such factors as the age level of your students.

Discipline Policies

When developing an effective discipline policy, keep it simple so that everyone can remember the components. Similarly, be sure the language is easily understood. Finally, focus on basic rights such as safety, learning, and respect. The sample below demonstrates how you can explain the philosophy of your school through a discipline policy.

Sample School Discipline Policy

At Maple Ridge School, we believe that people have certain rights and responsibilities. These rights and responsibilities are expressed as our core values and drive what we do on a daily basis. These core values apply to every member of our learning community. We believe that members of this learning community have:

The right to be safe and treated with response.

The right to learn.

The responsibility to be honest citizens.

The responsibility to be polite.

The responsibility to use time and resources wisely.

Source: Lucinda Johnston.

Johnston provides several guiding questions that are helpful as you consider revising or writing a policy.

Guiding Questions When Developing or Revising a Discipline Plan

What do we value and believe about the way people should treat one another?

What are the rights and responsibilities of everyone in this learning community?

How do we gather data about the core values of our school community?

What do we know about facilitating productive behavior?

How does our behavior affect our students?

What do students need to behave productively?

Keep in mind that you want a discipline policy that is effective and supports a positive school culture. Therefore, simply writing a list of statements, posting them in your school, and demanding compliance usually creates more problems than it solves. As with any other change initiative, seek input from all stakeholders, including students. Be sure everyone understands the reason for each part of the policy, and put the focus on school values rather than punishment. As one experienced principal explained, "The biggest lesson I've learned is not to develop a rigid policy to deal with an isolated situation."

Characteristics of Effective Discipline Policies

Information: Policies must be aimed at factual problems, not rumors. Gather accurate data before changing policy.

Involvement: All groups affected by a policy should be involved in creating it, including students.

Problem definition: Everyone will not agree on what constitutes undesirable student behavior. Define the problem as a first step toward solving it.

Flexibility: Rather than relying on a rigid system of penalties, policy should allow for different situations and prescribe different methods for different problems.

Communication: All students, parents, and school personnel should be aware of the school's discipline policy or student code of conduct. A readable, well-designed method of sharing the policy should be developed.

Consistent enforcement: If students are to cooperate with a discipline code, they must believe that they will be treated fairly.

Source: Adapted from "Student Discipline Policies," ERIC Clearinghouse on Educational Management, ERIC Digest no. 12 (ED 259455).

Share with Parents and Students

It is important to share the discipline policy with both parents and students. Be clear about what it means and about the process you will use to enforce the discipline policy. Many principals meet with groups of students at the beginning of every year to talk about the discipline policy.

Expectations Versus Rules

As you provide leadership in your school related to discipline, it is helpful to discuss the difference between expectations and rules. Expectations convey standards of behavior, whereas rules define misbehavior. People tend to live up or down to our expectations. Students need adults to have clear and consistent behavior expectations. Additionally, for student management to be most effective, adult behavior needs to be consistent with their expectations. For example, if a teacher expects students to be on time for class and ready to work, he or she must have work on the board and begin instruction immediately after the bell. Or, if an administrator expects students to be friendly and courteous, he or she must smile and greet students .

Helpful Hints

- Remember that expectations are different than rules. Be sure that most of the adults in your school agree with the behavior expectations.
- With staff, brainstorm ways to behave as if you expect productive behavior from people.
- Post expectations in prominent places throughout the school.
- Use the word "expect" when conveying expectations.
- Discuss ways to deal with students who do not live up to expectations.

Rules provide the framework for behavior in the school setting, and their presence allows the school community to engage in teaching and learning.

School rules are clearly value driven and should be stated in a positive format. School rules should support and reinforce the district behavior code. To be effective, they must be constantly and consistently communicated to members of the school community on a regular basis.

Questions to Guide Development of School Rules

Do our rules align with and reinforce our core values and beliefs?

Are our school rules fair and reasonable?

Can the rules be fairly and equitably applied to all members of the school?

Are our school rules appropriate for adults as well as students?

Do our school rules conform to district policy and constitutional requirements?

Should the policy emphasize punishment or prevention?

As with the development of your overall discipline policy, rules should be kept simple and few in number. Be sure to explain the values behind your rules, especially when someone has violated a rule. Review and reinforce school rules on a regular basis—don't assume that everyone remembers and understands the rules. And finally, as one student told us, "Don't have any stupid rules!" In other words, focus on things that are important rather than the trivial.

Classroom Rules

In addition to schoolwide rules, thoughtfully developed classroom rules ensure that teachers are able to maintain a classroom climate that is conductive to good teaching. In some schools, there are a few consistent rules used by all teachers, as well as two or three individual teacher-based ones.

Sample Classroom Policy with Common Rules

Common Rules

Begin bell work immediately when you enter the room.

Ask permission to speak or leave your seat.

Have your materials and supplies ready when the bell rings.

Individual Rules

Do not touch supplies or equipment until you are told to do so.

Show respect for the opinions of others.

Respect the privacy of my desk and work area at all times.

It is most effective when teachers and students work together to develop rules based on values. Also, whenever possible, state rules positively, as the sample classroom rules chart shows. However, there are times when a mandate is more effective, and in those times, it is appropriate to start with a negative. For example, "Do not touch items that don't belong to you" may be more effective than "Touch only items that belong to you."

A Final Note

Dealing with discipline issues can be frustrating and time-consuming. It can also distract you from your focus on learning. Create policies and procedures that reflect the values in your school and enlist the support of everyone in the school.

Skills for Principals

- Model personal and professional ethics, integrity, justice, and fairness, and expect the same of others.
- Behave in a trustworthy manner, using your influence and authority to enhance the common good.
- Involve families, teachers, and students in developing, implementing, and monitoring guidelines and norms for student behavior.
- Develop and monitor a comprehensive safety and security plan.

If You Would Like More Information . . .

Administrator's Complete School Discipline Guide: Techniques and Materials for Creating an Environment Where Kids Can Learn, by Robert D. Ramsey (Prentice Hall, 1994)

7 Steps for Developing a Proactive Schoolwide Discipline Plan: A Guide for Principals and Leadership Teams, by Geoffrey T. Colvin (Corwin, 2007)

Schoolwide Prevention Models: Lessons Learned in Elementary Schools, edited by Charles R. Greenwood, Thomas R. Kratochwill, and Melissa Clements (Guilford Press, 2008)

Discipline in the Secondary Classroom: A Positive Approach to Behavior Management (2nd ed.), by Randall S. Sprick (Jossey-Bass, 2006)

Information about promoting a positive peer culture is available from Educators for Social Responsibility, a national nonprofit organization that works with educators to implement practices that create safe, caring, and equitable schools: http://www.esrnational.org

This site includes information about Positive Behavioral Interventions and Supports: http://www.pbis.org/schoolwide.htm

This site contains tips for developing a schoolwide behavior management system: http://www.behavioradvisor.com/SchoolWide System.html

F

Finding the
Right People

The best executive is the one who has sense enough to pick good men to do what he wants done, and self-restraint enough to keep from meddling with them while they do it.

Theodore Roosevelt

Think About It

What is your experience with hiring personnel? Do you deal with a large turnover in your staff?

Hiring and retaining the right personnel is another important aspect of your job. When you have quality staff, your job as a leader is easier. When you have staff members who are uncooperative or ineffective, working with them can drain your time and energy. We're going to look at three aspects of working with personnel: finding the right people, keeping the right people, and finishing with the wrong people.

Finding the Right People

Last year, we met with a new principal who was hired to turn around a struggling school. At the end of his first year, 27% of his teachers left, either through retirement or resignation. His superintendent offered to pay his expenses to attend a recruitment fair to find new teachers, but he said he was too busy. If you are too busy to invest time in hiring the best people for your school, you are too busy! If there is a teacher shortage where you are, go out of your area to recruit. Don't settle for less than what is best for your students.

Hiring staff is often guided by district policies. The first thing you want to do is to check with the Human Resource Department about any procedures you must follow. This often includes developing a job description and list of duties.

As you hire, standardize the hiring process. Following a standard process ensures that you will treat everyone who applies in a uniform manner. Your district may have some of these procedures in place. If not, you will need to create them for your school.

First, develop your selection criteria. Each criterion should be relevant to the work to be performed and should be free of bias so that everyone is treated the same throughout the process. If you need someone who is bilingual, include that on your list. However, as you plan, differentiate between those skills or characteristics that are required and those that are simply desirable. All criteria must be relevant to the work, but you are likely to have some nonnegotiable items and some that you would like to have. Make sure you have addressed relevant employment laws (see chart) and that you document thoroughly. All criteria should be available for review.

Employment Discrimination Laws

Age Discrimination in Employment Act (1967): Age discrimination

Americans with Disabilities Act (1990): Protection for handicapped

Family and Medical Leave Act (1993): Provides leave for family medical needs

Title VII of the Civil Rights Act (1964): No discrimination on the basis of race, color, religion, gender, or national origin

Pregnancy Discrimination Act (1978): Protects the jobs of women who become pregnant and provides maternity leave

Next, create and use a protocol for interviews. The questions should be linked to your selection criteria, and they should be open-ended so as to provide in-depth information about the candidate. You might consider questions such as, "What do you see as your strengths related to this position?" "As you think about your past work experience, what has been your biggest challenge?" "Imagine you were offered the position and accepted it, and it is one year later. What was the best part of your first year, and what was your biggest challenge?" After you draft your questions, assess them to be sure you avoid any questions that are unlawful (see checklist).

Checklist for Assessing Interview Protocol

Unlawful Areas of Inquiry	Yes	No
■ Complexion or color of skin.		
■ Anything about applicant's religious beliefs, affiliation, church/parish/synagogue, pastor, or religious holidays observed.		
■ Applicant's gender, marital status, name or other information of spouse, or ages of children, if any.		
■ Whether applicant has a disability or has been treated for any of certain diseases.		
■ However, you may ask whether the applicant has any physical impairment that would affect the ability to perform the job for which the applicant has applied.		
■ Whether the applicant has ever been arrested.		
■ You may ask if the applicant has been convicted of a crime.		
■ Any previous name that the applicant has used.		
■ You may ask whether he or she worked for your organization under a different name (e.g., maiden name).		
■ Birthplace or birthplace of applicant's spouse; birth date or certificate of naturalization papers, and so on.		
■ Applicant's photograph before hiring. May ask if the applicant is a U.S. citizen, intends to become one, or has a legal right to work in the United States.		

Unlawful Areas of Inquiry	Yes	No
■ The applicant's native language. ■ You may ask which languages the applicant speaks and writes. ■ Questions or information about the applicant's relatives. Prior to employment, you may not even ask the name of a person to contact in case of emergency. ■ Clubs, societies, and lodges to which the applicant belongs. ■ You may ask the applicant whether he or she is a member of any organizations believed to be pertinent to the job.		

Finally, follow your process. In some cases, you may realize early in the interview that a person is not the best fit for the job. However, respect the candidate and the process and finish the interview. After you hire someone, be sure to send a written follow-up note to all candidates, notifying them that they did not get the job and thanking them for their interest in the position. A little courtesy goes a long way at this point; it never hurts to be nice, even to those you aren't hiring.

Keeping the Right People

Whether you have hired your own staff or inherited them from a former administrator, you want to keep the right people. Schools are basically people places, so it is important to nurture and cultivate talented employees and make them feel valued and part of the organization.

Steps to Create a "People-Oriented" Workplace

- See each person as an individual, as unique.
- Provide opportunities for each individual to assume responsibility.
- Remind individuals about the need for strict compliance with rules, but consider exceptions when appropriate.
- Create a place where people seek to learn from the experience and consider other alternatives rather than lay blame when things don't work out.
- Value listening and respecting varied points of view.
- Allow flexibility for people to teach or organize their classrooms in different ways.
- Provide opportunities for leadership to everyone.

As a leader, you have three keys that will help you unlock the door to employee satisfaction: effective communication, engagement in significant tasks, and valuing and respecting different points of view.

Effective Communication

Your first key to employee satisfaction is your ability to communicate effectively with your employees. When communicating, focus more energy on listening than speaking. Remember that much communication occurs through body language, so be attentive to nonverbal cues about meaning. Be aware of any power relationship (supervisor–supervisee, evaluator–evaluatee) that may be influencing the situation. Throughout the conversation, ask clarifying questions and probe for deeper meaning in response to any comments. Overall, focus on mutual problem solving and look for win–win solutions. And always identify next steps for each person, which will clarify each person's responsibilities.

Engagement in Significant Tasks

Next, quality employees are more likely to be satisfied if they are engaged in significant tasks. Identify meaningful ways to involve employees in school decision making rather than involving them in trivial decisions, such as the location of a copier. For all tasks, be clear in defining the task, the desired or required timeline, and any resources that will be provided.

Valuing and Respecting Different Points of View

Another key to retaining employees is your choice to respect points of view that differ from your own. Make it clear that you value freedom of expression, and reinforce that in every aspect of your job. When hearing unpleasant news, rather than reacting defensively, be open and probe for understanding by asking clarifying questions. Structure meetings and other activities to model openness, and use a decision-making process that requires exploration of alternatives and an analysis of advantages and disadvantages. Activities such as these will reinforce for your employees that you are open to differing perspectives.

Finishing with the Wrong People

Despite your best efforts, sometimes you will end up with the wrong person in a job. If you have tried to work with that person to become more effective, and it is still evident that you need a change, you have the uncomfortable job of terminating a person's employment.

Most Frequent Reasons for Dismissal

Inadequate performance: Relates to teaching skill, including classroom management

Immorality: Personal lifestyle issues or conviction on a felony

Insubordination: Failure to do what one is supposed to do; courts say that it must involve repeated acts in order to qualify for dismissal

Neglect of duty: Not being at an assigned place, particularly not supervising students or leaving students in a potentially dangerous situation

You will never enjoy this part of your job, but there are several things you can do to make this task easier.

Key Administrative Actions When Considering Dismissal

First, document everything, including all correspondence, classroom visits, and observations. Next, provide notice to the person about what needs to be changed or why you are recommending his or her dismissal. Be explicit in letting the employee know what he or she did not do and what needs to improve. The notice must be in writing, and you will want a record that the notice was provided. Allow time for the employee to improve. Provide the opportunity and time for the employee to modify his or her behavior in cases that do not involve immorality. Also, provide resources to support improvement. Generally, courts want to see that principals are working to support the improvement of performance and to give the employee resources he or she may need to improve, such as professional development, materials, or a peer coach. Finally, stay focused on the person's actions rather than allowing a negative person to drag you into a personal argument.

Reasons Principals Lose Dismissal Cases

The principal did not adequately document the case.

The policy that the staff member supposedly violated did not exist in writing.

The policy was ignored in other instances.

The principal was not clear enough in staff evaluations. For example, the principal failed to label the employee's performance as unsatisfactory

The principal acted before all due process requirements were met.

There is evidence that the administrator tried to intimidate the employee into resigning or retiring.

A Final Note

Ideally, you have the right people in place in every aspect of your organization. Focus your efforts on hiring and keeping the right people, but when you have a mismatch, finish with the wrong person in a way that is legal while preserving the dignity of everyone involved.

Skills for Principals

- Select and hire teachers and other staff who support the school's mission.
- Set appropriate performance standards for teachers and other staff.
- Understand the legal parameters for hiring and nonrenewal of teaches and other staff.
- Follow the school's or district's evaluation system.
- Provide professional development and other resources to support the improvement of staff performance.

If You Would Like More Information . . .

Building the Best Faculty: Strategies for Hiring and Supporting New Teachers, by Mary C. Clement (Scarecrow Press, 2000)

Cultivating High-Quality Teaching Through Induction and Mentoring, by Carol A. Bartell (Corwin, 2005)

101 "Answers" for New Teachers and Their Mentors, by Annette Breaux (Eye On Education, 2003)

"What Principals Look for When Hiring New Teachers": http://www.educationworld.com/a_admin/admin/admin257.shtml

"Principals Hold the Key to Teacher Retention": http://www.educationworld.com/a_admin/admin/admin411.shtml

"Always Strive to Be a Better You: Teacher Selection Counts: Six Steps to Hiring": http://www.educationworld.com/a_admin/columnists/hall/hall019.shtml

𝒢

Grading and Assessment

Told that the passing grade is a B or competence and that we will help you to get there, students do competent work. The lowest passing grade in the real world is competence. Why do schools accept so much less?

William Glasser

Think About It

How do the various stakeholders in your school feel about grades?

Grades are one of the most visible aspects of learning in schools. However, as you provide leadership to improve student learning, we must first consider the use of formative assessment. Then, we will turn our attention to grading policies.

Formative Assessment

With formative assessment, we continually assess student learning and use that information to plan future instruction. In 1998, Black and William provided a clear rationale that using formative assessment effectively raises standards. In 2004, they and other researchers provided a fuller explanation of formative assessment in *Working Inside the Black Box: Assessment for Learning in the Classroom:*

Assessment for learning is any assessment for which the first priority in its design and practice is to serve the purpose of promoting pupils' learning. It thus differs from assessment designed primarily to serve the purposes of accountability or of ranking or of certifying competence. An assessment activity can help learning if it provides information to be used as feedback, by teachers, and by their pupils, in assessing themselves and each other, to modify the teaching and learning activities in which they are engaged. (Black, et al., 2004)

W. James Popham (2008) in *Transformative Assessment*, describes four levels of implementation. These are useful to consider as you lead teachers in using formative assessment in their classrooms.

Popham's Levels

Level 1	Calls for teachers to use formative assessment to collect evidence by which they can adjust their current and future instructional activities.
Level 2	Deals with students' use of formative assessment evidence to adjust their own learning tactics.
Level 3	Represents a complete change in the culture of a classroom, shifting the overriding role of classroom assessment from the means to compare students with one another for grade assignments to the means to generate evidence from which teachers and students can, if warranted, adjust what they're doing.
Level 4	Consists of a schoolwide adoption of one or more levels of formative assessment, chiefly through the use of professional development and teacher learning communities.

Source: Popham (2008, p. ix).

Grading

Formative assessment is critical. So is evaluation, which is typically done through the assigning of grades as a designator of success in learning. In *Developing Grading and Reporting Systems for Student Learning* (2001, p. 51), Thomas R. Guskey and Jane M. Bailey describe six major purposes of grading and reporting:

1. Communicate achievement status
2. Provide information students can use for self-evaluation
3. Select, identify, or group students
4. Provide incentives for students to learn
5. Evaluate effectiveness of instructional programs
6. Provide evidence of students' lack of effort or responsibility

Each of these purposes is acceptable, but often we don't think about why we use grades. We simply assume that grades exist for a reason, and we may not challenge something that is accepted as the norm. One of the first steps you can take as a school leader is to initiate a conversation about the purposes of grading in your school.

Grading can be controversial. Concerns about grade inflation, an overemphasis on grades rather than learning, or incidents of cheating can negatively affect your school culture. However, there are ways to minimize the negative aspects of grading.

Minimizing the Negative Aspects of Grading

Recognize the value of grading to students, parents, and others.

Shift the emphasis to learning.

Provide clear guidelines.

Require quality work.

Communicate clearly.

Be patient.

Recognize Value

First, recognize why grades are valued. Some students want good grades because they are looking for outside affirmation that they are worthy. Others need a high grade point average for college admission or scholarships. Still others enjoy the competition of comparing themselves to others. Understanding why a student or parent is concerned about grading will help you and your teachers communicate more effectively.

Shift the Emphasis

Next, shift the emphasis to learning as opposed to grades. This takes time with teachers, students, and parents. However, the more you use formative assessment, the more you emphasize learning. One of the quickest and most effective methods we've used for minimizing a focus on grades is to have a large number of grades. That may seem counterintuitive, but when students receive a final grade based on one or two big items, such as tests or projects, it heightens anxiety. When a student has a larger number and wide variety of opportunities to demonstrate understanding, one bad grade does not matter as much. It's a choice of making every grade high stakes versus giving students multiple opportunities to succeed. Encouraging your teachers to use a wider range of assessments and grades supports higher levels of learning.

Provide Clear Guidelines

It's also important to provide students with clear guidelines and a detailed rubric for all projects and key assignments. This supports your goal of clear communication with all stakeholders.

Require Quality Work

Next, as the quotation opening this chapter points out, we should require that all students complete work at an acceptable level. Many of our graduate students work in school systems that do not allow zeroes. The purpose of that policy is to keep students from falling so far behind that they can never catch up. In some cases, teachers are directed to assign a minimal grade, such as a 60, rather than assigning a zero. That can send mixed messages to students and create resistance from teachers. Bob Heath, former principal of Sullivan Middle School, collaborated with his teachers to find an alternative.

> What we have discovered here is that just teaching more isn't what raises the bar. It's making kids do the work that they are hesitating or refusing to do. We created more time in our daily schedule for students to get face-to-face with teachers to complete that work. If they don't turn something in, they meet with that teacher to do the assignment. They are not going to get away with just not doing it. We have to break the cycle of passive resistance a lot of kids have toward doing work. It's developed over years but we have to say "No." We are going to make you do the work. We will not just give you a 60. We will make you do the work to earn the authentic grade."

Bob's suggestions are excellent, but they are working in part because it is a schoolwide expectation that all students will complete work at an acceptable level.

Communicate Clearly

Provide clear communication about grades and grading policies. Ideally, teachers will meet together by grade levels, teams, or departments to agree on consistent grading policies. If homework "counts," students and parents need to know that. Ms. Keith, for example, does not grade homework, but if a student neglects to turn it in, she takes points off the final grade. She believes that students need to do homework for the sake of learning, and then their grades on tests will be higher because of the homework. That is fine, but she never told her students. When Jorge received a C, despite test grades that averaged to a B, his parents called to question the overall grade. They finally understood but commented to the principal, "It would have been okay if we had just known." The last thing you want to hear from a student or a parent is, "If I had just known . . . "

You may choose to require all teachers to provide a written grading policy. This does not mean you must dictate the terms of the policy. Teachers should have that choice. However, it is reasonable and prudent to call for all teachers to have a written explanation of what and how they grade, and provide reminders to students of the policies.

Sample Grading Policy Components

Description of types of assessments (tests, projects, homework, etc.)

Description of weight of assessments (percentage of grade, etc.)

Overall expectations for completion (e.g., "not yet" policy for projects)

Procedures for makeup work (when student is absent)

Opportunities for extra help (regularly scheduled days and times)

Be Patient

Finally, be patient. Discussions or change initiatives related to grades can be controversial. It seems as though grading is the last great barrier of freedom for teachers. However, grades are an outward reflection of what you and your faculty believe about learning. It is important to consider what that means to your staff and what changes are necessary. And, although teachers want and need some flexibility, it's important to be consistent on major facets of grading. If your initial attempt to discuss grading doesn't go as smoothly as you would like, take time to reflect and readjust rather than giving up.

General Principles

There is not an ideal grading policy. Grading policies and procedures must be tailored to your school community. Variations are needed depending on the grade levels served, your school's philosophy on assessment and evaluation, and stakeholders' perspectives on grading. However, as you lead teachers in considering grading policies, there are general principles to consider.

Principles for Evaluation and Grading

Use a variety of assessments.

Make sure the type of assessment matches your purpose.

Clearly explain what you are evaluating and the purpose of the evaluation.

Create and provide explicit guidelines for grading.

Build in opportunities for students to succeed.

A Final Note

Assessment and grades make an impact on student learning. It is important to consider how they reflect the philosophy and culture of your school. Balancing the use of formative assessment to inform instruction with authentic grading policies will have a positive impact on your students.

Skills for Principals

- Develop and use aligned, standards-based accountability data to improve teaching and learning.
- Work with teachers to identify multiple sources of information about teaching and learning.
- Ensure that grading and assessment strategies do not promote inequitable curricular or instructional practices.
- Communicate with families and caregivers about grading and other assessment systems.

If You Would Like More Information . . .

Rigor Is Not a Four-Letter Word, by Barbara R. Blackburn (Eye On Education, 2008)

Rolling the Elephant Over: How to Effect Large-Scale Change in the Reporting Process, by Pamela Brown Clarridge and Elizabeth M. Whitaker (Heinemann, 1997)

Transformative Assessment, by W. James Popham (Association for Supervision and Curriculum Development, 2008)

Developing Grading and Reporting Systems for Student Learning, by Thomas R. Guskey and Jane M. Bailey (Corwin, 2001)

Transforming Classroom Grading, by Robert J. Marzano (Association for Supervision and Curriculum Development, 2000)

"Leading to Change: Effective Grading Practices," by Douglas B. Reeves: http://pdonline.ascd.org/pd_online/mi/el200612_reeves.html

"Do Schools Give 'Equal Grades for Equal Work'?": http://www.educationworld.com/a_issues/issues105.shtml

"Beginning the Change Process: One District's Look at Grading," by Barbara R. Blackburn: http://coe.winthrop.edu/blackburnb/Blackburn/beginning.pdf

H

Helpful Resources

Whatever we learn has a purpose and whatever we do affects everything and everyone else, if even in the tiniest way. Why, when a housefly flaps his wings, a breeze goes round the world; when a speck of dust falls to the ground, the entire planet weighs a little more; and when you stamp your foot, the earth moves slightly off its course. Whenever you laugh, gladness spreads like the ripples in a pond; and whenever you're sad, no one anywhere can be really happy. And it's much the same thing with knowledge, for whenever you learn something new, the whole world becomes that much richer.

Norton Juster, *The Phantom Tollbooth*

Think About It

What are the key resources you turn to when you need new information?

Several years ago we heard a speaker discussing the information overload in our information-rich society. He said the amount of information available to us doubles every 24 hours, and the amount available would only increase in the future. With the Internet, e-mail, and other print and electronic databases, the amount of available information can be overwhelming. As a principal, it's impossible to be an expert in every topic.

Instead, it's important to know the key resources so that you can find the information you need when you need it.

We've provided specific topic-based resources at the end of each chapter of this book. However, in this chapter, we want to provide you with a short guide to the top resources available to you. Each provides up-to-date, credible information for a changing world.

Groups You Should Know

First, you will find a list of organizations that deal with the major content areas. Each provides a wealth of resources geared toward its specific audience. Most sites include links to the national standards for that content area.

Recommended Content Associations

National Association for the Education of Young Children, http://www.naeyc.org

National Council of Teachers of Mathematics, http://www.nctm.org

International Reading Association, http://www.reading.org

Council for Exceptional Children, http://www.cec.sped.org

National Science Teachers Association, http://www.nsta.org

National Council for Social Studies, http://www.ncss.org

National Council of Teachers of English, http://www.ncte.org

There are also several organizations that provide specific information that is helpful to principals. They include membership groups related to your specific level as well as organizations that provide resources about teaching, learning, and professional development.

Recommended Professional Associations for Principals

National Association of Elementary School Principals,
   http://www.naesp.org
National Association of Secondary School Principals,
   http://www.nassp.org
National Middle School Association, http://www.nmsa.org
Association for Supervision and Curriculum Development,
   http://www.ascd.org
American Association of School Administrators, http://www.aasa.org
National Staff Development Council, http://www.nsdc.org

There are 10 nonprofit agencies and educational laboratories that we recommend. These provide research-based resources geared to specific topics.

Recommended Resources on Educational Research

North Central Regional Education Lab, http://www.ncrel.org—
   educational technology
Southwest Educational Development Lab, http://www.sedl.org—
   family and community involvement
WestEd, http://www.wested.org—assessment of educational
   achievement
Annenberg Institute for School Reform,
   http://www.annenberginstitute.org)
Southern Regional Education Board, http://www.sreb.org
Learning Point, formerly the Midwest Regional Educational Lab,
   http://www.learningpt.org
Northwest Regional Educational Lab,
   http://www.nwrel.org—reengineering schools for improvement
SouthEastern Regional Vision for Education (SERVE),
   http://www.serve.org—expanded learning opportunities
Mid-Continent Research for Education and Learning,
   http://www.mcrel.org—standards-based instructional practice
Clearinghouse on Educational Policy and Management, University of
   Oregon, http://www.eric.uoregon.edu—focus on school leadership
   and issues of interest to school leaders (law, negotiations, finance,
   reform, choice)

Web Sites

The number of Web sites dedicated to educational topics grows everyday. For easy access, we recommend that you bookmark the ones most useful to you. In addition to these, those on your "must visit regularly" list should include your state department of education site as well as any state organizations related to your role.

Recommended Web Sites

Education Week, http://www.edweek.com

The Principals' Partnership, http://www.principalspartnership.com

International Center for Leadership in Education,
    http://www.leadered.com

Children's Defense Fund, http://www.childrensdefense.org

The Principals' Page, http://www.principalspage.com

Center for Adaptive Schools, http://www.adaptiveschools.com

Turning Points Comprehensive School Reform Model,
    http://www.turningpts.org

Coalition of Essential Schools, http://www.essentialschools.org

Looking at Student Work, http://www.lasw.org

Scholastic Administrator, http://www.scholastic.com

Web-Based Tools

A related set of resources are the tools available to you via the Internet. In Chapter J: Juggling Priorities, we provide sample strategies from Frank Buck, a former principal who won the 2007 Marbury Technology Innovation Award as the top central office staff member in Alabama. We've worked with Frank, and we turned to him for an updated list of Web-based tools that can streamline your work.

Frank Buck's Recommended Tools

Blogs: These are my windows to the world. I maintain a personal blog to communicate about my passions, time management and organization, another to communicate with employees within the school system, and a third to communicate with the community and rest of the world. I use Blogger (http://www.blogger.com). For those in education, Edublogs (http://www.edublogs.com) is an outstanding free source.

RSS (Really Simple Syndication): Time does not permit me to check each of the blogs I like to follow. A free program called "intraVnews" (http://www.intravnews.com) sends the posts straight to my Outlook Inbox.

iGoogle (http://www.google.com/ig): I think of it as the "dashboard" I see every time I boot my computer at the office or at home. I like being able to access my most common bookmarks and other tools from any computer in the world.

Del.icio.us (http://del.icio.us/): Being able to save favorites and bookmarks has always been a great feature of a Web browser. Being able to see my bookmarks from any computer and share them with those who have similar interests takes the concept to a whole new level.

GoogleDocs (http://docs.google.com): This tool gives me a "parking place" on the Web for documents I want others to view and for documents I want others to be able to edit.

Jott (http://jott.com) and reQall (http://www.reqall.com): With one touch of a speed-dial key, you can speak a message that will be transformed into an e-mail reminder for yourself or a message for someone else.

TeacherTube (http://www.teachertube.com): Now, the presentations we create for our own purposes can be seen by everyone.

PhotoBucket (http://photobucket.com): Instead of posting a large number of individual photos to our blogs, we can now produce a slideshow in a very small space.

Animoto (http://animoto.com): This ridiculously easy tool takes a collection of pictures and turns them into a flashy presentation.

Podcasting: This tool basically lets you create your own radio program, which can then be uploaded to a blog or Web site. Getting really good with this tool is an upcoming project for me. "Audacity" (http://audacity.sourceforge.net) is a free program that provides a great beginning for anyone interested in podcasting.

Books

In spite of the growth of electronic resources, we still believe in the power of a book. First, you'll find a list of education books, then our favorites related to leadership.

Recommended Books About Education

Shaking up the Schoolhouse: How to Support and Sustain Educational Innovation, by Phillip C. Schlechty (Jossey-Bass, 2001)

Closing the Achievement Gap: A Vision for Changing Beliefs and Practices (2nd ed.), by Belinda Williams (Association for Supervision and Curriculum Development, 2003)

Learning by Doing: A Handbook for Professional Learning Communities at Work, by Richard DuFour, Rebecca DuFour, and Thomas Many (Solution Tree, 2006)

Courageous Conversations About Race, by Glenn Singleton and Curtis Linton (Sage, 2006)

Results Now: How We Can Achieve Unprecedented Improvements in Teaching and Learning, by Mike Schmoker (Association for Supervision and Curriculum Development, 2006)

School Leadership That Works, by Robert J. Marzano, Timothy Water, and Brian A. McNulty (Association for Supervision and Curriculum Development, 2005)

Enhancing Student Achievement: A Framework for School Improvement, by Charlotte Danielson (Association for Supervision and Curriculum Development, 2002)

Classroom Instruction That Works: Research-Based Strategies for Increasing Student Achievement, by Robert J. Marzano, Debra J. Pickering, and Jane E. Pollock (Association for Supervision and Curriculum Development, 2001)

Sixteen Trends, Their Profound Impact on our Future: Implications for Students, Education, Communities, and the Whole of Society, by Gary Marx (Educational Research Service, 2006)

Leadership and Sustainability: System Thinkers in Action, by Michael Fullan (Jossey-Bass, 2005)

No Excuses: Closing the Racial Gap in Learning, by Abigail Thernstrom and Stephan Thernstrom (Simon & Schuster, 2003)

What Great Principals Do Differently, by Todd Whitaker (Eye On Education, 2002)

From Good Schools to Great Schools: What Their Principals Do Well, by Susan Penny Gray and William A. Streshley (Corwin, 2008)

Recommended Books About Leadership

The 8th Habit: From Effectiveness to Greatness, by Stephen R. Covey (Free Press, 2004)

Good to great: Why Some Companies Make the Leap—and Others Don't, by Jim Collins (HarperBusiness, 2001)

The World Is Flat: A Brief History of the Twenty-First Century, by Thomas L. Friedman (Farrar, Straus and Giroux, 2005)

The Tipping Point: How Little Things Can Make a Big Difference, by Malcolm Gladwell (Little, Brown, 2002)

Judgment: How Winning Leaders Make Great Calls, by Noel M. Tichy and Warren G. Bennis (Penguin, 2007)

Leading at a Higher Level: Blanchard on Leadership and Creating High Performing Organizations, by Ken Blanchard (Prentice Hall, 2007)

The 21 Indispensable Qualities of a Leader: Becoming the Person That People Will Want to Follow, by John C. Maxwell (Thomas Nelson, 1999)

The Go-Giver: A Little Story About a Powerful Business Idea, by Bob Burg and John David Mann (Penguin, 2007)

Learning to Lead: A Workbook on Becoming a Leader (3rd ed.), by Warren Bennis and Joan Goldsmith (Basic Books, 2003)

The Fifth Discipline: The Art and Practice of the Learning Organization, by Peter M. Senge (Doubleday, 2006)

A Final Note

In a world of ever-increasing resources, in which all sorts of information is readily available, your task is filtering through all the options to find what you need. As Barbara's dad says, "Education is figuring out what to do when you don't know what to do." Part of your role is figuring out where to find what you need when you don't have the information you need.

Skills for Principals

- Recognize the need to stay current on state and national issues affecting education.
- Read contemporary materials on leadership and schooling and use the reading to shape your work as a school leader.
- Model the importance of accessing up-to-date information about effective teaching and learning practices.
- Provide support, time, and resources for staff to continuously improve their practice.

If You Would Like More Information . . .

State-of-the-Art Fact Finding: New Ways to Find the Information You Need, Now, by Trudi Jacobson and Gary McClain (Dell, 1993)

Research Strategies: Finding Your Way Through the Information Fog, by William B. Badke (iUniverse, 2004)

Google: http://www.google.com

Descriptions of meta-search engines: http://www.lib.berkeley.edu/ TeachingLib/Guides/Internet/MetaSearch.html

Educational Resources Information Center: http://www.eric.edu

George Lucas Educational Foundation provides an array of teaching materials and resources with a technology focus: http://www. glef.org

I

It's All About Instruction

I have witnessed how education opens doors, and I know that when sound instruction takes place, students experience the joys of new-found knowledge and the ability to excel.

Daniel Akaka

Think About It

How much of your time is allocated for instruction? What is the most pressing instructional issue in your school?

A recent poll conducted by the National Association of Secondary School Principals (NASSP) found that only 16% of principals' time was spent on instructional issues, while more than three-quarters (78%) was devoted to student supervision or management concerns.

The responsibility for improving instructional quality resides with school principals. Many principals, because of the size or complexity of their schools, find it a challenge to allocate the time to work with their staff, but improving instruction is a key function of school leaders. The principal plays an important role in creating a climate in which conversations about instructional effectiveness are common and part of the everyday operation of the school.

There are many ways that principals can focus the work of school personnel on improving instruction. Most involve establishing a mechanism for teachers to work collaboratively and to have conversations about student learning and about their teaching. There are several tools that principals can use to support this work.

Tools

Establish norms of collaboration.

View instruction from a student's perspective.

Strategically focus on instruction.

Close the achievement gap.

Provide a rigorous learning environment.

Establish Norms of Collaboration

Fundamental to the work of schools is creating a climate in which teachers and other staff are comfortable talking about complex and difficult issues—one in which it is safe to pose tough questions, to question current practice, and to suggest alternatives. Bob Garmston and Bruce Wellman described norms as "skills that become the 'normal' behavior in a group" (1999, p. 37).

In some groups the norm is silence. In others it is open, honest dialogue. Garmston and Wellman identified seven norms of collaboration that create a climate characterized by a spirit of inquiry and openness to new and creative ideas.

Seven Norms of Collaboration

Pausing
Paraphrasing
Probing
Putting ideas on the table
Paying attention to self and others
Presuming positive intentions
Pursuing a balance between inquiry and advocacy

More information about the norms and guidelines for their use are available at the Web site of the Center for Adaptive Schools (http://www.adaptiveschools.com).

View Instruction from a Student's Perspective

A second strategy is to gather data to lead instruction by viewing instruction from the perspective of a student. An effective technique for gathering information on the curricular and instructional experiences of students is to conduct a shadow study. Shadow studies involve selecting students at random and following them throughout their day.

The protocol, originally developed by the NASSP, suggests charting the experience of students at five- to seven-minute intervals. This allows the observer to show the ebb and flow of activities during the day. Spending the entire day with a student and documenting his or her experience provides interesting insights into the student experience. Of course, students quickly figure out that something is going on. The best approach is to talk with the student and assure him or her that you are not gathering information about them to report to the office.

Shadow Study Observation Form

Time	Specific Behavior (Five- to Seven-Minute Intervals)	Comments and Impressions

After gathering the data, the information can be used as a springboard to launch conversations at the faculty or departmental level about the experience of students. The patterns that emerge across students and across classrooms can provide helpful guidance to improve instructional quality.

Another way to obtain the students' view of instruction is to conduct focus groups or form a Principal's Advisory Group of students. If students trust you, and they believe that you want to listen to them, students will give you frank feedback about schools. One of our favorite questions to ask students is, "If you were in charge of the school, what would you change?"

In *Rigor Is Not a Four-Letter Word* (2008), Barbara shares her experience with a student responding to this question. The school had good test scores and used those scores to place students in tracked classes. The principal and faculty believed that all classes were of high quality and were sufficiently challenging for each student. Gabrielle, a sixth-grader in the school, responded, "For people who don't understand as much . . . [they should] be in higher-level classes to understand more [because] if they already don't know much, you don't want to teach them to not know much over and over."

The principal and teachers were taken aback. They had no idea that students in the school viewed the lower-level classes as less challenging. The feedback from Gabrielle prompted them to reevaluate their curriculum and instruction.

Strategically Focus on Instruction

There are four specific strategies that you can use to focus your school on instructional improvement.

Four Strategies

What principals talk about becomes important.
Tell stories about improvement.
Focus the conversation.
Use staff meetings differently.

First, *what principals talk about becomes important.* Principals who introduce the idea of improving instruction into their day-to-day conversation with teachers find that it subtly sends a message to teachers about the importance of instruction.

During conferences with teachers following classroom observations, a principal from suburban Hartford asked questions such as, "When you design a lesson what things to do think about? What data about your students' prior learning do you use to guide your lesson design?" Such questions suggest that teachers should be thoughtful in their planning. Rather than "telling" teachers to do this, the message is conveyed through these structured conversations.

Next, *tell stories about improvement.* A principal in suburban Phoenix told "turn around" stories that described significant changes that occurred in the learning of an individual student. In each case, he linked the students' success to the efforts of a specific teacher who had either changed his or her instruction or had gone "over and above" to help the student learn.

Third, *focus the conversation.* At the end of one school year, an elementary school principal gave every teacher a copy of *Classroom Instruction from A to Z.* She invited them to read it over the summer and to return in the fall ready to share and use their learning. On the day teachers returned, they organized into study groups of those who had read the book and talked about its implications for their work. Throughout the year, teachers chose one chapter and shared during a faculty meeting how they had implemented the strategies.

Fourth, *use staff meetings differently.* A principal in Oregon converted monthly staff meetings into an opportunity for professional development. Working with the School Improvement Team, he identified topics of interest, located print and online resources, established faculty study teams, and used the time formerly devoted to staff meetings as a time for the groups to meet, develop plans, and prepare their recommendations to the entire staff. After a few months, the groups began to meet on their own at lunch and before or after school. He reported that they were "as enthusiastic as I've ever seen them about school improvement."

Close the Achievement Gap

We cannot conclude our discussion of instructional leadership without addressing one of our most critical challenges: closing the achievement gap. There are two reasons that principals should lead the charge to close the achievement gap. First, it is the right thing to do. Every single child who enters our building deserves the right to learn and have the opportunity to succeed. Second, we are held accountable for closing the gap by the No Child Left Behind Act and by state achievement initiatives.

In *Closing the Achievement Gap: A Vision for Changing Beliefs and Practices* (2003), Belinda Williams identified four needs of students.

Needs of Students

1. Access to challenging curriculum and instruction
2. High-quality teachers
3. High expectations
4. Extra support

The needs are clear; the challenge is how to respond.

Provide a Rigorous Learning Environment

Those needs are best met when you and your faculty provide students with a rigorous learning environment. Let us be clear about our definition of rigor. First, center your attention on quality, not quantity. Rigor is not about increasing the number of homework problems assigned. True rigor does more with less, preferring depth over breadth. Next, rigor is not just for your advanced students. Rigor is for every student in your building. That includes your students who are at risk of failure, your students with special needs, and your students for whom English is not their native language. Finally, the heart of authentic rigor is learning, not punishment. It is about growth and success, not failure. Your focus should be on how you can inspire your teachers to lead their students to higher levels of rigor in a positive, productive manner through expectations, support, and instruction.

> "Rigor is creating an environment in which each student is expected to learn at high levels, each student is supported so he or she can learn at high levels, and each student demonstrates learning at high levels." (Blackburn, 2008)

Provide a Personalized Learning Environment

It is important that students feel connected to their school. There is strong evidence that when a student has a supportive relationship with a single adult in school, he or she is more likely to stay in school and to achieve at higher levels.

In elementary school, the classroom teacher often serves that function. In many middle and high schools, an advisory or advocacy program is often included. Typically the program consists of a small group of students assigned to one teacher who monitors their progress in school and talks with them about academic and social issues.

Some schools create a more personalized environment by organizing into smaller units. In Chapter M (Managing Schedules), we discuss how one elementary school organized classrooms into multigrade wings. Many middle schools organize into interdisciplinary teams in which every teacher on a team teaches the same students. The teachers work together to create a learning environment that is supportive of their students.

Many large high schools are adopting a small "school-within-a-school" model. Students and teachers are organized into small units, often built on a curricular theme. The goal is to create a more personalized setting in which students are well known by teachers and to develop a supportive connection with school. Support staff such as school counselors and assistant principals are often assigned to each small school.

These organizational models simply create the potential for a more personalized environment. It is essential that teachers get to know their students well and commit to building personal relationships with each student.

Role of Principals

There are endless suggestions for closing achievement gaps and increasing rigor in schools. Given these challenges, where do you start? Begin by hiring only the most skilled teachers (see Chapter F: Finding the Right People). Evaluate and work with those teachers who are less skillful (see Chapter Q: Quality Teacher Evaluations).

Work with staff through professional development (see Chapter P: Professional Development and Chapter W: Working Together) to identify high expectations and to change behavior so that words and actions convey those expectations. Also work with teachers and district staff to modify curriculum and improve instructional expertise focused on adding rigor and challenge to the program.

Collaborate with community partners to secure additional resources to support the instructional program and before and after school programs for students. Commit to co-curricular programs that support the academic needs of students, and provide support activities that enhance the academic rigor of the school's program. This might include organizing academic games or restructuring the schedule to allow for required remediation or tutoring during the regular school day.

A Final Note

It is easy to get caught up in the endless stream of issues related to school management. However, providing leadership for effective instruction is critical and must take priority. Additionally, creating an rigorous learning environment for all students is important and will help close the achievement gap.

Skills for Principals

- Develop a shared vision of high performance for every student.
- Mobilize staff to achieve the school's vision.
- Work to develop a coherent and rigorous curriculum.
- Create a personalized, motivating, and engaging learning environment for every student.
- Provide appropriate instructional supervision.
- Develop the instructional capacity of teachers and other staff.
- Utilize assessment and accountability systems to monitor student progress.

If You Would Like More Information . . .

Closing the Achievement Gap: A Vision for Changing Beliefs and Practices (2nd ed.), by Belinda Williams (Association for Supervision and Curriculum Development, 2003)

Unfinished Business: Closing the Racial Achievement Gap in Our Schools, edited by Pedro A. Noguera and Jean Yonemura Wing (Jossey-Bass, 2006)

Closing the Achievement Gap—Reaching and Teaching High Poverty Learners: 101 Top Strategies to Help High Poverty Learners Succeed, by Tiffany Chane'l Anderson (iUniverse, 2004)

Rigor Is Not a Four-Letter Word, By Barbara R. Blackburn (Eye On Education, 2008)

NEA Foundation: http://www.neafoundation.org/closingthegap_resources.htm

Minority Student Achievement Network—resources for ensuring high academic achievement for students of color: http://www.msanetwork.org

The Education Trust provides many resources for closing the achievement gap including research articles and presentations: http://www2.edtrust.org

The North Central Regional Education Laboratory, a regional research lab, provides ideas about how to address achievement gaps among students: http://www.ncrel.org/gap/

J

Juggling Priorities

One slip and down we fall, it seems to take no time at all.

Jason Womack

Think About It

If you were completely effective, efficient, and balanced, what would your life be like?

The principalship involves an incredible array of responsibilities and tasks. Managing them can be complex and seemingly impossible. At times, it can become overwhelming, and you can find yourself caught up in necessary but less important tasks. However, principals have developed a number of strategies to help organize the tasks and devote their time and energy to their most important priorities.

Managing the tasks is important because most principals want to be seen as "staying on top" of things. Their reputation as an effective manager often relates directly to their ability to juggle multiple priorities and accomplish multiple tasks at the same time. Let's look at a three-step process that can help you with this juggling act.

Three-Step Process to Achieve Balance

1. Assess where you are and where you want to be.
2. Begin with a mental adjustment.
3. Create structures to support your vision.

Assess Where You Are and Where You Want to Be

The first step is to recognize the strengths and challenges of your current situation. One principal we interviewed was so overwhelmed, she said, "I don't think I can make a list. It will make it seem worse!" That's not true. You may think you don't have time for this step, or you may not want to think about all the challenges, but it is critical in order to make progress.

Assessment of Current Situation

Strengths	Challenges

As we continued to work with the principal, her list of strengths was longer than she thought. She had an efficient, highly skilled administrative assistant, she utilized an effective system for logging and returning calls, and she was known for meeting deadlines. Her list of challenges was long, but she realized that things weren't as out of control as she perceived.

The second part of this process is to create a vision of where you want to be. Take a few moments to imagine a day in which you are relaxed and productive. You might go back to your response to the "Think About It" question at the beginning of the chapter. Now, create a statement that describes your vision and write it on an index card.

Sample Vision Card

> Within three years this school will be the highest performing school in the district, with no differences among subgroups of students.

Begin with a Mental Adjustment

Next, adjust your thought process. Our thoughts drive our feelings and actions. If you want to make a change, start with how you think about what you are doing.

Negative Thoughts	Positive Thoughts
I'll never have an empty inbox.	I'm cleaning out my inbox everyday.
I'll never get caught up.	Today, I choose to make progress on my task list.
100% of our students can't meet standards	I'll make a positive impact on one child today.
It's impossible to keep everybody happy	Every interaction I have with people will be sincere regardless of their behavior.

Focus on the positive progress you are making each day, whether it is effectively delegating a task or choosing to take time to mentor a potential leader. It's also helpful to review your vision on a regular basis. Carry your index card with you, and post your vision where you can see it, such as on a sticky note attached to your computer screen.

Create Structures to Support Your Vision

Finally, create a set of regular, consistent structures that ensure you will attain your vision. There is not a perfect strategy—except the one that works for you. However, there are strategies that have been effectively used by other principals.

Sample Strategies

"Tickler File": Many of the responsibilities and tasks occur annually. Education is cyclical. A ticker file is a way of creating a reminder about the tasks to be anticipated, planned for and accomplished. For example, a high school principal will need to confirm graduation plans annually, and an elementary principal will need to conduct kindergarten roundup annually. Some people use a set of file folders labeled by month and include items in the folder that remind them of the tasks to be accomplished that month. One principal created an electronic file to accomplish the same task. Some people use a daily ticker file instead of a monthly file.

Develop a filing system: Use colored file folders to distinguish tasks. One principal used a red folder to identify things requiring her signature, a green folder to hold new correspondence, yellow for pending activities, and blue for completed work and papers in need of filing. Such a system can work with a secretary or administrative assistant to organize tasks.

Use a journal: A number of administrators maintain a running journal to take notes in meetings and create a "to do" list. This ensures that everything is in one place rather than on multiple pieces of paper or multiple sticky notes. It makes it easy to look back and find ideas and tasks that emerged in earlier meetings. May be either digital or paper

Maintain a single calendar: Nothing can be more confusing and lead to missed commitments than maintaining multiple calendars.

Handle it only once: To the extent possible, handle any correspondence or e-mail only once. Unless it requires additional thought or planning, respond, delegate, or file.

Plan weekly or monthly: Many principals find it helpful to look at the "big picture" and plan either weekly or monthly. Taking this big look at tasks allows the leader to make decisions about the allocation of time.

Delegate: Be comfortable delegating tasks to people who have the knowledge and skill to complete them.

Organize your digital life: Arrange computer files and documents, so that information can be easily retrieved. Use a flash drive or external hard drive to back up work routinely.

Use all available e-mail tools: Delete if not needed, save if appropriate and documentation is required, forward to someone else, or complete the task.

Use e-mail tools: Check e-mail at set times, not all the time. If you can, respond when you first read the message. Handle them all as a group—start with the first and move through them until complete. Use descriptive subject lines to identify the substance of the message. Set up a signature line including name and contact information. Keep messages short to ensure that the response is focused.

Keep your focus: Turn off the automatic notification on your e-mail program. When it beeps, it only distracts you from your work.

Break large projects into small parts: Define the goal and create a series of tasks. Often smaller tasks are easier to accomplish, and this helps to move the project along.

Establish norms around access: Everyone wants an "open door," but a literal open door can lead to fragmentation. Identify a quiet time each day to respond to e-mail. Don't reinforce the idea that you respond the minute you receive a message. Establish norms around interruptions. Work with school clerical staff to protect time.

A Final Note

Juggling the various priorities and tasks can be challenging. However, by setting a vision, adjusting your perspective, and creating a set of structures to support your goals, you can become more effective in your job.

Skills for Principals

- Value a high-quality curricular and instructional program above all else.
- Recognize the importance of balancing managerial and instructional tasks.
- Develop a method for establishing priorities.
- Implement systems to deal with routine managerial tasks.
- Understand that the work is never done.

If You Would Like More Information . . .

Get Organized! Time Management for School Leaders, by Frank Buck (Eye On Education, 2008)

Getting Things Done: The Art of Stress-Free Productivity, by David Allen (Viking, 2001)

Taming Your Gremlin: A Surprisingly Simple Method for Getting Out of Your Own Way, by Rick Carson (Quill, 2003)

"Principals Offer Practical, Timely 'Time Management' Tips": http://www.education-world.com/a_admin/admin/admin436_a.shtml

This newsletter from the Michigan Principals Fellowship and Coaches Institute contains tips for time management: http://www.aypsupport.org/December_Newsletter2007.pdf

K

Keys to Successful Public Relations

Our lives begin to end the day we become silent about the things that matter.

Martin Luther King, Jr.

Think About It

What strategies or programs are currently in place in your school to communicate with the public?

Public relations is one of the most important roles of a school leader. As we consider this topic, you might also think about the idea of advocacy rather than public relations. Advocacy is what you do when you are advocating, or actively supporting a cause. Public relations is how you relate to the public. To be effective, you will do both.

As you regularly communicate with school stakeholders—students, parents, teachers, and the community—they learn key messages about the school's programs, policies, and practices. It is an effective way to create a positive image of the school and to share the school's successes. We'll look at five specific areas to address:

1. Sharing your knowledge about your issues
2. Presenting yourself well to the media
3. Understanding opposition
4. Building a network
5. The final point: editing yourself

Sharing Your Knowledge about Your Issues

The cornerstone of your public relations and advocacy efforts is your ability to share your knowledge about issues. There are two key tools that you should have in your advocacy toolbox: the One-Page Fact Sheet and the Elevator Speech.

One-Page Fact Sheet

The One-Page Fact Sheet helps you organize the important facts and points of your issue. It can be used as a handout, and it will give you the necessary background information as well as the added confidence to discuss the issue. A One-Page Fact Sheet is essential for your preparation. One page is your limit. Most decision makers want the basic facts and don't want wasted time. The limit also enables you to keep your message focused.

Key Points in a One-Page Fact Sheet

- Clearly define the issue.
- State your position on the issue.
- Clarify what you want the decision maker to do.
- Define five talking points in order of importance.
- Provide two references to support issue.
- Make the sale with a closure statement.

Elevator Speech

There are occasions when you have a brief opportunity to make personal contact with a key decision maker. In those cases, you should be prepared to give a personal story on your connection to education and the importance of your issue. The elevator speech is a 30–60-second story that includes three elements:

1. Your name and your job
2. Your key issue
3. What you would like the decision maker to do

You should practice telling your story and explaining why you care about this issue with another person. This will give you confidence when you have a golden opportunity: a chance or planned meeting with a key decision maker.

Presenting Yourself Well to the Media

At some point, you will likely be required to deal with the media, whether it is your local newspaper or some form of electronic media. Don't be taken by surprise; anticipate that you will need to communicate with the media and plan appropriately. Preparation is your friend, especially when there is a crisis situation (see Chapter U: Under Pressure).

Tips for Dealing with the Media

- Preparation is your best friend—learn as much as you can about the reporter, the show, and the audience.
- Establish your communication goals for each interview.
- Determine two or three key points to make to reach your goal.
- Speak in "memorable language."
- Learn and use the "bridging technique." Redirect the interview to your key points.
- Practice, practice, practice. Practice on camera if possible
- Do not wear clothes or use mannerisms that distract from your message.
- Forget jargon, now and forever.
- Make sure that the mind is in gear before the mouth travels.
- Look at the reporter when answering questions; turn to the camera when delivering a key point.
- Steady eyes suggest honesty; blinking or darting eyes suggest nervousness and dishonesty.
- Anticipate questions and have answers ready. Once the interview is scheduled, try to figure out what questions the reporter might ask.
- Relax.

Understanding Opposition

As we work with the public, and especially the media, we must recognize the different groups of people around us. You probably know people who will support you on any new initiative, as well as those who won't (see Chapter N, New Ideas, New Challenges). When dealing with public relations, it is crucial to anticipate opposition. Christopher Kush, in the *One-Hour Activist* (2004), categorizes four types of opposition:

1. Natural opposition
2. Fiscal opposition
3. Strange and unanticipated opposition
4. Friendly fire

There are those you know who will oppose you, those who are concerned about financial issues, those who unexpectedly oppose you, and those who support you but who may say or do something that is considered "friendly fire." Understanding that you will meet these opponents allows you to prepare to deal with them.

First, don't react negatively. That puts you on the defensive and makes you less credible. Next, acknowledge the opponent's perspective. This shows you are listening. Third, analyze the opponent's argument. Look beneath the surface to understand his or her perspective. Finally, counteract the opponent's arguments, using personal stories and reasons that match his or her goals and needs whenever possible. You may not always convince your opponent, but you are likely to be more effective than simply ignoring him or her.

Building a Network

To be truly effective, you need to build a network of people who can help you communicate. Remember, communication is a two-way street, so this group will serve two purposes: to help you understand how stakeholders in various groups perceive a situation, and to help you communicate your message. There are actually several layers of this strategy. For example, if you lead a large school, you may use an existing leadership team to assist you in this area. In addition, you may want a network for parents and another one for the business community. Or you may want one network that incorporates all those groups.

One model is the Key Communicator Network, developed by the National School Public Relations Association. That organization recommends a series of steps for building a network and leading that group.

As you work with stakeholders, there is one key point to remember: As the principal, you are the face of the group. Share responsibility, but don't forget that in the eyes of the community, you are responsible for getting things done and for sharing reliable and accurate information. Never create a situation in which you compromise your beliefs about honesty and trustworthiness.

Building a Key Communicator Network

- Bring together a small group of trusted people who know the community. Together, identify the people whom others listen to. While the bank president may be an opinion leader, so might the barber, cab driver, bartender, or supermarket checkout clerk.
- Create a workable list of people to invite to join your network. Make sure that all segments of the community are represented.
- Send a letter to the potential members, explaining that you want to create a new communications group for your school to help the community understand the challenges, successes, and activities of your school. In the letter, invite the potential members to an initial meeting and include a response form.
- Make follow-up phone calls to those who do not return the response form, especially those who will be most important to have in your network.
- Start the initial meeting by explaining that those in the audience have been invited because you see them as respected community members who care about the education that students are being provided. Also, point out that you believe schools operate best when the community understands what is taking place and becomes involved in providing the best possible learning opportunities for students. Then, describe the objectives of a Key Communicator Network:
  - to provide network members with honest, objective, consistent information about the school;
  - to have the network members deliver this information to others in the community when they are asked questions or in other opportunities; and

> - to keep their ears open for any questions or concerns community members might have about the school. Those concerns should be reported to the principal or person in charge of the network so communication efforts can deal with those concerns. (It's always best to learn about concerns when one or two people have them instead of when 20 or 30 are vocally sharing them with others.)
> - Ask the invitees for a commitment to serve on the network and find out the best way to communicate with them, i.e. email, fax, and telephone.
> - Establish a Key Communicator Network newsletter specifically for these people. After the first year, send out a short evaluation form to see how the network is working and might be improved.

For more information about Key Communicator Networks, contact the National School Public Relations Association (http://www.nspra.org) to purchase a copy of *A Guidebook for Opinion Leader/Key Communicator Programs.*

The Final Point: Editing Yourself

Finally, whether you are communicating in writing or verbally, it's important to process your thoughts and to revise your message. Think of yourself as your own editor: After you have organized your thoughts, go back and edit to ensure your content is clear and concise and communicates your message as effectively as possible. Use the following tips for editing (adapted from Lew Armistead, *LA Communications*) to help you begin.

Tips for EDITING

E	Edit from the perspective of your audience. Think of how they will hear your message and revise to match their needs.
D	Delay. After one revision, put it aside, wait, and then come back to it. It's easy to become too close to your writing; you need some space.
I	Identify the desired result. Can you state this? If not, you are missing the call to action. Give your audience an idea of the appropriate response.

T	Trust yourself—in addition to spell check. The computer won't catch everything. Don't assume it will.
I	Invite a second opinion. Have a colleague, friend, or assistant check for errors. They may see something you have missed.
N	Narrow your choices. One trap is providing too much information. Keep your focus, and keep it simple.
G	Get feedback. If you have time, ask trusted stakeholders to provide feedback on the content. Ask them to identify your key points and your desired result. If they can't, then your message isn't clear.

A Final Note

Working with the public is a necessary part of your job. You are the face of your school, and your school is a part of the community. Therefore, you should always be prepared to communicate with those around you and advocate for your school.

Skills for Principals

- Understand the importance of planned community relations.
- Develop a system for regular communication with school constituents, including families and community members.
- Provide honest, truthful communication above all else.
- Communicate and act from shared vision and mission so that the community understands, supports, and acts on the school's vision and mission.
- Uses communication strategies to develop family and local community partnerships.

If You Would Like More Information . . .

Selling the Invisible: A Field Guide to Modern Marketing, by Harry Beckwith (Warner Books, 1997)

You, Inc.: The Art of Selling Yourself, by Harry Beckwith (Warner Business Books, 2007)

The Tipping Point How Little Things Can Make a Big Difference, by Malcolm Gladwell (Little, Brown, 2002)

The One-Hour Activist: The 15 Most Powerful Actions You Can Take to Fight for the Issues and Candidates You Care About, Christopher Kush (Jossey-Bass, 2004)

The Anatomy of Buzz How to Create Word-of-Mouth Marketing, by Emanuel Rosen (Doubleday/Currency, New York, 2000)

"Public Relations 101: How-To Tips for School Administrators": http://www.educationworld.com/a_admin/admin/admin123.shtml

These two articles from the American Association of School Administrators provide simple tips for working with the media:

"How to Deal with the Media": http://www.aasa.org/publications/content.cfm?ItemNumber=3939; and "Productively Engaging the Media": http://www.aasa.org/publications/content.cfm?ItemNumber=8468

L

Looking at Student Work

One of the things we have tried to do is work on a culture to increase student achievement for all students. I saw in the last school I worked in, the enormous benefit of looking at student work so we can tweak our curriculum.

Catherine Richard

Think About It

How do you and your faculty use student work as a tool for school improvement?

One powerful way to learn about your school's instructional program and to improve the educational experience of students is to look at authentic student work. In many schools, teams of teachers, either at the departmental, course, or grade level, examine the work of students as a way to clarify their own standards for student work, to strengthen common expectations for students, or to align curriculum across faculty.

Looking at student work is a complex task that significantly alters the norms of a school. It necessitates a climate in which faculty are comfortable sharing their work with colleagues and revealing artifacts of their classroom

80

practice. The Annenberg Institute for School Reform suggests several preliminary steps.

Steps to Begin Looking at Student Work

- Talk together about the process and how to ensure that it is not evaluative.
- Identify ways to gather relevant contextual information (e.g., copy of assignment, scoring guide or rubric).
- Select a protocol or guideline for the conversation that promotes discussion and interaction.
- Agree on how to select work samples.
- Establish a system for providing and receiving feedback that is constructive.

Although there are many purposes for looking at student work, we are going to address four specific ones in this chapter:

1. Aligning expectations with standards
2. Developing consistent expectations
3. Analyzing strengths and weaknesses
4. Using student work as a tool for accountability in professional development

Aligning Expectations with Standards

One purpose for looking at student work is to align teachers' expectations with standards. The first step this requires is to define "high quality." Rubrics are an effective way to determine expectations for quality. However, if you don't have anything for comparison, you may unknowingly lower your standards. Using benchmarks allows you to frame the conversation through a lens of neutral standards rather than limiting the perspective to personal opinions.

The Southern Regional Education Board (SREB) offers detailed descriptions of proficiency levels tied to the National Assessment of Educational Progress (NAEP) test levels for students preparing to enter high school. One of the findings from research conducted by the SREB is that many teachers expect advanced students to perform at the proficient level and on-grade level students to perform at a basic level of competency. The following charts show sample expectations for students leaving the eighth grade.

Making Inferences and Predictions
(Reading/Language Arts)

Basic	Proficient	Advanced
■ Identify an author's stated position ■ Make simple inferences about events and actions that have already occurred, characters' backgrounds, and setting ■ Predict the next action in a sequence	■ Use evidence from text to infer an author's unstated position ■ Identify cause and effect in fiction and nonfiction ■ Predict a character's behavior in a new situation, using details from the text ■ Formulate an appropriate question about causes or effects of actions	■ With evidence from a nonfiction piece, predict an author's viewpoint on a related topic ■ Describe the influence of an author's background upon his or her work ■ Recognize allusions

Source: Southern Regional Education Board, 2004.

Gather, Organize, Display, and Interpret Data
(Math/Algebra I)

Basic	Proficient	Advanced
■ Make and read single bar graphs, single line graphs, and pictographs ■ Read and interpret circle graphs ■ Find the mean, median, mode, and range of sets of data	■ Read and make line plots and stem-and-leaf plots ■ Collect and display data for given situations ■ Make, read, and interpret double bar, double line, and circle graphs	■ Formulate survey questions and collect data ■ Evaluate statistical claims in articles and advertising ■ Analyze different displays of the same data

Basic	Proficient	Advanced
■ Plot points on a coordinate grid	■ Determine when to use mean, median, mode, or range ■ Determine and explain situations of misleading statistics	

Source: Southern Regional Education Board, 2004.

Describe Sound and Light in Terms of the Properties of Waves (Science)

Basic	Proficient	Advanced
■ Describe the electro-magnetic spectrum ■ Demonstrate the characteristics of sound and light waves ■ Explain the effect of different media substances on wave trans-mission.	■ Relate the electro-magnetic spectrum to practical applications ■ Examine and relate character-istics of sound and light to wavelength, amplitude, and frequency ■ Research why different energy forms require a medium	■ Draw conclusions about natural phenomena based on the electromag-netic spectrum ■ Research and summarize the effects of surfaces on light and sound reflection and absorption ■ Research product designs that impact sound transmission

Source: Southern Regional Education Board, 2004.

There are a variety of other sources for standards for all grade levels, including the "New Standards" Performance Standards of the National Center on Education and the Economy's (NCEE, http://www.nc ee.org) and an online set of national content standards compiled by the Mid-Continent Regional Education Laboratory (http://www.mcrel.org/standards-bench marks/). Choose the national standards that are most helpful for your use.

Developing Consistent Expectations

It's helpful to gauge expectations with published standard expectation levels, but it's also important to simply sit down with other teachers and administrators to discuss expectations. One way to start the conversation is to choose a standard assignment that students complete, such as writing a short essay. Share copies of the paper with a group, and ask everyone to assess it. Because everyone participates, each teacher actually assesses a paper from each of the other teachers. If you do this by department, grade level, or team, you will probably have about five papers to assess. Meet to discuss the results. It's likely that some teachers will be more rigorous, and others less so. However, as you talk about how you determine quality, you'll come to consensus about your expectations.

We recommend that you begin by structuring or guiding meetings among teachers of the same subject and grade level. Over time, build to conversations across grade levels. Ask questions of teachers of higher grades such as, "What do you expect students to know before they come into your class?" "From your perspective, what are the overall strengths students bring into your classroom? What are some areas that students struggle with?" Then, meet with teachers one grade level below each teacher's level to discover new information to help guide instruction for the coming year.

Barbara was working with one district to address consistency across grade levels. A specific area of concern was homework. Teachers at one of the middle schools explained that they assign less homework to sixth-graders because "They are coming from elementary school and must adjust to our higher expectations." However, when she visited the feeder elementary school, fifth-grade teachers told her, "We always assign homework and expect it to be completed. We want them to be ready for middle school." Because the teachers at each school had never met to discuss expectations, the sixth-grade teachers had less rigorous requirements but didn't realize it. The teachers and principals met together to ensure expectations were aligned.

Analyzing Strengths and Weaknesses

A third way to use student work is to analyze strengths and weaknesses in your instructional program. For example, if your school is focusing on integrating writing across all areas of the curriculum, over the course of a year, students' writing samples in classes other than English/language arts should show improvement.

A middle school in suburban Chicago, for example, had cross-content teams look at samples of student work. The school focused on improving the quality of written expression, created a rubric based on state standards for assessing written assignments, and then met in teams to analyze the work. During the meetings, a teacher presented the assignment, the writing rubric, and samples of student work. The team then discussed the strengths and weaknesses of the student work and identified way that each member of the team could strengthen their writing assignments.

A Utah high school committed to improving the quality of students' analytical skills. Math teachers designed a set of "anchor" assignments to be completed by all students. The focus was on solving problems by describing the steps that would be used to arrive at a solution. Once a month, the math teachers worked together to review the students' work and to identify ways that they could improve the quality of their instruction.

Using Student Work as a Tool for Accountability in Professional Development

Finally, looking at student work is one of the best tools a principal can use to ensure accountability with professional development (see Chapter P: Professional Development). We worked with one school to focus on effective instructional strategies. Teachers participated in a session that modeled several strategies. Then, they were asked to choose one strategy that they believed would be effective in their particular classroom and use it at least once during the month. Upon our return, none of the teachers had tried a strategy in their classrooms. For the next month, the principal reinforced his belief that it was important to try a new strategy, and he asked to see samples of students' work for the strategy. All of the teachers tried an activity. As the principal said to us, "I thought I was trusting my teachers when I didn't ask for the follow-up. Some of my best teachers said they were busy and didn't think I cared if they used the strategies, especially when I didn't ask them about it. Two years later, I don't have to ask to see student work; they bring me samples to show me what they are doing in the classroom."

A Final Note

Student work is one of the most authentic measures of what is happening in your school. By systematically looking at student work samples, you can make decisions that will have an impact on the instruction in your school.

Skills for Principals

- Monitor teaching and learning to develop the capacity for and commitment to high expectations for all students.
- Develop a shared understanding of rigorous curriculum and standards-based instructional programs.
- Work with teams to analyze student work, monitor student progress, and ensure that curricular and instructional programs meet diverse student needs.
- Supervise instruction so that all students have a high-quality, rigorous academic experience.

If You Would Like More Information . . .

Looking Together at Student Work (2nd ed.), by Tina Blythe, David Allen, and Barbara Schieffelin Powell (Teachers College Press, 2008)

The Facilitator's Book of Questions: Tools for Looking Together at Student and Teacher Work, by David Allen and Tina Blythe (Teachers College Press, 2004)

Collaborative Analysis of Student Work, by Georgea M. Langer, Amy B. Colton, and Loretta S. Goff (Association for Supervision and Curriculum Development, 2003)

Several online resources are available to support this work. The Looking at Student Work Web site (http://www.lasw.org), supported by the Annenberg Institute, provides more than 10 protocols that can be used for conversations about student work. The site also provides a detailed description of the rationale for examining student work as well as lots of supporting materials.

This article by Barbara R. Blackburn describes one district's initiative to look at student work: http://coe.winthrop.edu/blackburnb/Blackburn/authentic.pdf

M

Managing Schedules

A revised schedule is to business what a new season is to an athlete or a new canvas to an artist.

Norman Ralph Augustine

Think About It
How would you rate the effectiveness of your current schedule? Are there adjustments you would like to make?

Creating and managing the school schedule can be one of the most time-consuming tasks facing a principal. It's easy to focus on the logistics of the schedule, but an effective schedule or organizational pattern is just a tool to accomplish other things. There are four basic principles for building an effective schedule.

Basic Principles

- Schedules reflect a school's values and priorities.
- Most effective schedules are anchored in a shared vision.
- A quality schedule emerges when teachers and administrators work together in its design.
- Without clear goals, the schedule is merely a plan for organizing teachers and students; when guided by goals, the schedule becomes a powerful tool to positively affect teaching and learning.

An effective organizational model is a powerful tool to improve instruction. Through the process of developing or adjusting the schedule, you can facilitate or promote collaborative work, help with interdisciplinary links, and create varied instructional design. Remember, you can schedule anything; you just can't schedule everything in the same schedule. It's all about priorities.

Before you begin to design a school schedule, you will want to check and see whether your district or state has any requirements that might shape the schedule. For example, some states require a certain number of minutes of instruction in some content areas. Other things that may affect the schedule are facility constraints and workload limits included in employee contracts.

Starting the Conversation

The first step is to have a conversation about the schedule with key stakeholders. In this step, it's important to begin with clearly identified goals. Clarity of goals builds support for a new schedule and narrows the alternatives to be considered.

Next, organize the conversation around a series of questions. For example, what data do we have that we should consider changing the schedule? Given a new schedule, how do we want to allocate time based on needs of students? Do some subjects need additional time for instruction?

Throughout the conversation, value collaboration. Participation in planning builds support and serves as a form of professional development and it builds capacity for a successful implementation. Finally, provide a balanced review; investigate all options and have a thorough discussion of advantages and disadvantages of all models that are considered.

Scheduling Options

The approach to scheduling varies among elementary, middle, and high school. Approaches that fit one school may not work in another. What is most important is to consider your school's program and its students. Select the approach that helps to improve the educational experience of your students.

Elementary School Schedules

Most elementary schools are organized into self-contained classrooms. In some schools, the upper elementary grades may be organized around departmental subjects. An issue that faces all elementary school principals is how to schedule special classes such as art, music, and physical education. The preference of many elementary teachers is to have uninterrupted time for reading and mathematics instruction in the morning. This creates a conflict because all special classes cannot be scheduled in the afternoon.

Factors to Consider
When Scheduling Special Classes

Priority for uninterrupted instructional blocks
Providing planning time by scheduling across the week
Need to provide common grade level planning time
Special teachers who may be shared with other schools

Another way that some elementary schools organize classes is to place all lower elementary classes in one wing of the school and all upper elementary classes in another. This allows each wing to focus on the developmental needs of those students. It also permits greater collaboration among teachers at each grade level.

Yet another strategy used in some schools is to place a class or two from each grade in each wing. This facilitates teacher interaction among the grades and eases grouping and regrouping of students for some instruction.

Another approach to organizing elementary schools to provide greater content-specific instruction is the parallel block schedule. This schedule allows teachers to teach a single content area and to develop instructional skills for a specific content area. Teams of teachers share students among the content areas. A parallel block schedule also allows students to be grouped based on instructional ability and facilitates grouping and regrouping so that students are not necessarily tracked in all content areas.

In the following example, having four teachers at a grade level permits two teachers to teach reading, language arts, and social studies and two to teach math and science. Students in each grade go to "special" classes at the same time, providing teachers with common planning time.

	1	2	3	4	5
Tch A Rdg/LA/SS	Rdg/ LA	Rdg/ LA	S	Rdg/ LA	Rdg/ LA
Tch B Rdg/LA/SS	Rdg/ LA	Rdg/ LA	P E	Rdg/ LA	Rdg/ LA
Tch C Math/Sci	Math/ Sci	Math/ Sci	C A	Math/ Sci	Math/ Sci
Tch D Math/Sci	Math/ Sci	Math/ Sci	L S	Math/ Sci	Math/ Sci

As with all scheduling models, adaptations are needed to fit the specific needs of your school.

Middle and High Schedules

Middle and high schools offer additional scheduling challenges because of the number of specialized courses offered and the complexity of the curriculum. There is not a one-size-fits-all approach; rather, you will need to find the approach that best matches the needs of your school.

Six Scheduling Approaches

Traditional fixed period
Block schedules
Alternating schedules
Rotating schedules
Dropped schedules
Trimester Schedules

Source: Williamson (2009).

Fixed Period Schedule

In a traditional fixed period departmental schedule, classes are generally of equal length and meet every day for a semester or year.

Fixed Period Schedule

1
2
3
4
5
6

Block Schedules

Block schedules provide longer instructional blocks, which can be used for instructional flexibility. Teachers often have greater choice in instructional strategies, releasing energy and creativity often restricted in a traditional schedule. Blocks also have a positive impact on school climate. There are often fewer class changes and fewer classes each day, reducing stress for both teachers and students.

Here is an example of a four-by-four block schedule, with four classes each semester.

	Semester 1	Semester 2
1	English	Algebra 1
2	Spanish 1	Concert Band
3	Phys Ed	Economics
4	Earth Science	Speech

In some schools the four-by-four block schedule looks different. Each day has four classes, and they alternate from day to day. This example shows one week. The next week, Classes 5–8 would meet on Monday, Wednesday, and Friday, while Classes 1–4 meet on Tuesday and Thursday.

	Mon	Tues	Wed	Thu	Fri
8:00–9:30	1	5	1	5	1
9:35–11:05	2	6	2	6	2
11:05–11:35	Lunch				
11:35–1:05	3	7	3	7	3
1:10–2:40	4	8	4	8	4

Alternating Schedules

In an alternating schedule, each class does not meet every day. You may alternate days or alternate semesters. In this scenario, having fewer classes each day provides longer instructional blocks, with the same benefits mentioned earlier. Alternating models vary the class meetings on any given day. Most often, an alternating schedule simply alternates the classes from day to day all year.

Rotating Schedule

In a rotating schedule, classes actually rotate from day to day throughout the week. A Maryland middle school uses this schedule, and teachers rave about the benefits of working with students at different times during the day. They value the different perspectives that it provides about students and their learning.

Mon	Tue	Wed	Thu	Fri
1	2	3	4	5
2	3	4	5	6
3	4	5	6	1
4	5	6	1	2
5	6	1	2	3
6	1	2	3	4

Dropped Schedules

In a dropped schedule, a class is dropped and another activity occupies the time. In the following sample, a Michigan high school replaces two classes a week with a seminar period. During the seminar, teachers work with students on a variety of study skills; it provides an opportunity for advising students on school issues. The "dropped" classes vary from week to week assuring that no single class is always impacted.

Mon	Tue	Wed	Thu	Fri
1	1	1	1	1
2	Seminar	2	2	2
3	3	3	3	3
4	4	4	4	4
5	5	5	Seminar	5
6	6	6	6	6

Trimester Schedules

Finally, the trimester schedule is a model increasingly used by high schools and some middle schools to provide students with more classes. The school year is divided into three equal parts, with courses scheduled accordingly.

	Fall	Winter	Spring
1	Algebra 1	Algebra 1	English 1B
2	English 1A	Biology	Biology
3	Phys Ed.	Spanish 1B	World History 1A
4	Spanish 1A	US History	Phys Ed
5	Band	Band	Band

Rubric for Effective Schedules

Again, the question is not which schedule is best. The question is which schedule is best *for your situation*. An effective schedule is a tool that allows you and your faculty to accomplish your goals. The rubric on the following pages will assist you as you assess your progress toward effective scheduling.

Rubric

Redesigning your school's schedule usually involves teachers and other school personnel. The primary goal is to improve instruction and provide teachers with greater control over and flexibility in the instructional program.

We're found that it is important to consider both process issues and instructional issues when thinking about the schedule. Few schedules are described as "perfect." This rubric can be used to both assess your current schedule and provide a design for continued growth.

The rubric on the following pages will assist you as you assess your progress toward effective scheduling.

**Rubric for Scheduling
Process Issues**

	High	Medium	Low
Participation	Teachers are actively involved in selecting the design of the schedule.	Limited involvement of some teachers in design of the schedule.	Teachers are not involved in selecting the design of the schedule.
Decision Making	The adoption of a new schedule design is made using an agreed upon decision-making process.	The decision-making process involves some teachers and other school personnel.	Adoption of a new schedule is problematic because it was decided by the administration.
Use of Data	Multiple sources of data including data about student learning are used to guide selection of a new schedule design.	Limited data are used to establish the design of the schedule.	Little or no data is gathered and used to guide decisions about the design of the school schedule.
Professional Development	A multiyear professional development program focused on instructional design supports adoption of a new schedule.	Some professional development is provided.	No professional development is provided to support adoption of a new schedule.

Rubric for Scheduling
Instructional Issues

	High	Medium	Low
Long Instructional Blocks	The school day provides long instructional blocks that can be used to meet the instructional needs of students.	The schedule includes some instructional blocks in some subjects.	Instructional time is divided into fixed period classes that minimize options for flexible instructional practices.
Presence of Common Planning Time	The schedule provides common time during the school day for teachers who work together to meet and plan instruction.	Some teachers have common planning time with other teachers at their grade or in their content area.	The schedule provides little or no common planning time for teachers who share students or teach a common grade or content area.
Grouping and Regrouping	Teachers may group and regroup students within grades or teams to address individual learning needs.	The schedule provides limited opportunity to group and regroup students.	The organization of teachers and classes inhibits the regrouping of students for instruction.
Use of Space	The school allots space to provide teachers with various size rooms that can be used for the instructional program.	There is some limited flexibility in use of space.	Little or no space is provided for teachers to use for various instructional activities other than single classrooms.
Teachers Decide Use of Time	Individual teachers or teaching teams make decisions about the use of their instructional time.	Some flexibility is built into the schedule for teachers to allocate instructional time.	The schedule does not allow teachers to flexibly use classroom instructional time.

A Final Note

Managing the school schedule can present challenges. However, if you view the schedule as a tool, you can use it to facilitate growth in collaboration and to accomplish the instructional goals of your school.

Skills for Principals

- Be open to change and model collaboration that improves teaching and learning.
- Make a quality educational experience for students the school's first priority.
- Organize the school to maximize the focus on a quality learning experience for students.
- Align resources (time, people, and space) to achieve the school's vision and goals.

If You Would Like More Information . . .

Elementary School Scheduling: Enhancing Instruction for Student Achievement, by Robert Lynn Canady and Michael D. Rettig (Eye On Education, 2008)

Scheduling to Improve Student Learning, by R. Williamson (National Middle School Association, 2009)

Information about trimester schedules is available from http://www.trimesters.org

Several research briefs about scheduling are available from the Principals' Partnership.

Trimester Schedules: http://www.principalspartnership.com/TrimeserSchedulesApr08.pdf

Block Schedules: http://www.principalspartnership.com/block scheduling.pdf

Scheduling for Small High Schools: http://www.principals partnership.com/masterschedule.pdf

Research on block scheduling is available from the University of Minnesota's Center for Applied Research and Educational Improvement: http://cehd.umn.edu/carei/blockscheduling/

N

New Ideas,
New Challenges

It is not the strongest of the species that survive, nor the most intelligent, but the one most responsive to change.

Author unknown,
commonly misattributed to Charles Darwin

Think About It

How do your teachers react to a proposed change?

There is an old saying, "The only person who likes change is a baby with a wet diaper." As a principal, you have likely dealt with someone who was not supportive of a proposed change. However, one of your chief functions as a principal is to lead change, even when you do not have the support of everyone in your school.

Ways People Respond to Change

People respond to change in one of three ways. Approximately 5% are early adopters who are eager to embrace almost any innovation. Another 5%

will never adopt change; nothing can get them to embrace an innovation. The remainder are those people who can be moved toward support for change if they are given sufficient time and information. In this chapter, we will focus on that 90%. How can you help those who are reluctant to change become part of positive progress?

Reasons for Resisting Change

Think of the last time you wanted to implement a change in your school. You probably heard a variety of responses similar to the following.

Comments Resisting Change

"I don't see why we need to do this."

"You (the principal) already made up your mind to change."

"My opinion doesn't count."

"This is just one more thing to do."

"How does this relate to what we are already doing?"

"We've tried this before and it didn't work."

People resist change for one of two reasons. They don't see the value of the change, or they do not believe they can be successful with the change. Each of the comments above fits into one of those categories. As a principal, it is imperative to understand these two reasons in order to respond accordingly.

Value

Just as students ask, "Why do we need to learn this?" teachers ask, "Why do we need to do this?" The question may be spoken or unspoken, directed to you or discussed in the teachers' lounge, but it is always at the forefront of any proposed change. To support an innovation, teachers must understand the value of the change.

As you think about how the innovation you are considering is of value, it's important to remember Maslow's hierarchy. When you adopt a new innovation, you may find that many employees revert to a lower level. They are concerned about basic needs (materials, training, schedule, etc.) and must understand how those will be met before they can address the higher levels of the hierarchy.

Maslow's Needs

Need as Identified by Maslow	Example of Staff Needs
Aesthetic Need (self-actualization)	Attention to the needs of students first
Need for Understanding Need for Knowledge	Focus on the developmental needs of students Professional development: ▪ Program models ▪ Planning skills ▪ Curriculum ▪ Instructional strategies ▪ Diversity issues ▪ Assessment strategies
Esteem Needs Belonging Needs	Will I be successful? Will I be valued? Will I fit in? How do the new social and work norms align with my beliefs?
Security Needs Survival Needs	Where will I be working? Where will my room or office be located? What will my work look like? Who's making these decisions? Will I continue to have a job? Will I have the skills for the job? Will I have sufficient and appropriate materials?

Source: Adapted from Maslow (1968).

Success

The second facet of resistance is the desire to succeed. Most people have high competence needs, and they believe they are successful in their current work. Any change is viewed through a lens of how the person can continue to be successful. Therefore, you should provide appropriate support to help develop the skills to be successful with new innovation.

How to Respond

Despite the appearance of stubbornness, most people don't resist just to resist; they resist because they lack information about an innovation or because they don't have adequate time to embrace it. Time and information are the two keys to overcoming resistance. First, you must provide time for most of those involved to adopt and learn about the new innovation. Second, you will need to provide sufficient information about how the innovation will impact people's work. Remember, everyone needs to feel successful. There are five strategies you can use to smooth the transition process and overcome the resistance to change.

Strategy 1:
Build Relationships and Involve People

The first strategy for overcoming resistance to change is to build relationships with all stakeholders and involve them in the proposed change. During this step, it's important to identify everyone who will be affected by the change. It's easy to overlook someone who is not directly involved in a project but whose support will be critical in the future. Ensure their cooperation by involving them early.

Possible Stakeholders or Constituent Groups

Families

Community members

Community service agencies (e.g., medical, mental health)

Citizens without children in the schools

Teachers and other school personnel

Teachers from feeder schools

City agencies (e.g., Recreation Department)

Strategy 2:
Establish a Common Base or Context

As you work with all constituency groups, establish a common base of information for the proposed change. One of stumbling blocks to progress is a lack of information; therefore, be sure everyone has a sufficient knowledge base to discuss and move ahead with the project. Although this can happen through a large group discussion, such as in a faculty meeting, it is usually more effective to provide multiple opportunities for conversation in smaller groups prior to a discussion with the entire faculty.

- Individually, make notes about current conditions in your school community. Identify critical issues and the evidence to support their inclusion.
- With colleagues, discuss the conditions you identified, develop a ranking or priority for the concerns, cite the evidence, and agree on trends affecting your school community. Discuss and identify the implications for each item for schools.

Concerns-Based Discussion Chart

Concern	Ranking	Evidence	Implications

Strategy 3:
Provide a Clear, Concrete Result

This strategy is often assumed, and therefore it may be overlooked. In order to overcome resistance to change, teachers need to see a clear, defined outcome. You should always be able to answer one question: "If we are successful implementing _____, we will know it because we will see _____." In other words, what would success look like? This does not mean you must develop the vision yourself without any input; the most lasting visions are shared ones. However, for any proposed change, it is important to have a clear vision, and share that vision with all constituent groups.

Strategy 4:
Have a Structure That Supports Success

Fourth, you need to build a structure that supports success. This does not mean you must know every step prior to the innovation. However, you do need a way to clearly identify each step, a proposed time frame, roles and responsibilities, and necessary resources. Using a Process Chart such as the one that follows is helpful to ensure that everyone understands each step and his or her role in the process. Remember that you structure should incorporate the elements of value and success, such as providing appropriate professional development that will help teachers feel more successful with the proposed change.

Process/Change

Strategy	Time Frame	Person(s) Responsible	Resources Needed

Strategy 5:
Focus and Refocus the Conversation

Finally, keep the conversation focused. It is easy, particularly in a large group discussion, to become distracted by personal agendas. In a recent workshop, a leadership team was planning a remediation class for at-risk learners. Two teachers began to argue about classroom space and their own scheduling preferences. As we noted earlier, people revert to lower levels of Maslow's hierarchy when they are concerned about change. In this instance, the group had already developed a solution to both those issues, but the two teachers continued to complain. The principal reminded the group of the rationale for the remediation classes: to positively affect student learning for their neediest students, particularly second-language learners, by providing additional time for learning. She reframed the conversation, and the group was able to move forward. In addition to having a vision for change, you must continually keep that vision as a focus. And at times, you will need to use the vision to refocus the conversation.

Helpful Ideas for Communicating
when Conflict is Present

- Share data and descriptions, not value judgments or interpretations.
- Use active listening skills.
- Focus on the present, not what has been or might be.
- Agree when those of a different viewpoint are right.
- Own your ideas and feelings; use "I" as much as possible.
- Guard against too much openness.
- Make constructive use of silence; provide and demand time to think.
- Delay making judgments or decisions.
- Explain, do not defend.
- Be sensitive to nonverbal clues and messages.
- Recognize and request rewording of questions that have no answers, are rhetorical, or include commands or directions.
- Avoid the use of superlatives and absolutes (most, best, always, never).
- Assume the motives of others are honorable.
- Discourage preaching and teaching behaviors.

A Final Note

Finally, remember that overcoming resistance to change is possible. The vast majority of your teachers can and will respond appropriately if they see the value of the innovation and if they believe they will be successful. It is your job to help them do so.

Skills for Principals

- Work collaboratively with school constituents to develop a shared vision and mission for the school.
- Promote continuous and sustained improvement.
- Collaboratively develop and implement plans to achieve the school vision and mission.
- Work with constituents to identify indicators of school success.
- Monitor those indicators, gather data about progress, and use those data to guide decisions about school improvement.
- Nurture a school culture that is trusting, has high expectations, and is focused on a high quality learning experience for all students.
- Anticipate emerging trends at the local, regional, state and national levels so that the school can respond appropriately.

If You Would Like More Information . . .

Change Leadership: A Practical Guide to Transforming Our Schools, by Tony Wagner, Robert Kegan, Lisa Laskow Lahey, Richard W. Lemons, Jude Garnier, Deborah Helsing, Annie Howell, and Harriette Thurber Rasmussen (Jossey-Bass, 2006)

Schools That Change: Evidence-Based Improvement and Effective Change Leadership, by Lew Smith (Corwin, 2008)

The Human Side of School Change: Reform, Resistance, and the Real-Life Problems of Innovation, by Roberts Evans (Jossey-Bass, 1996)

Asking the Right Questions: A School Change Toolkit: http://www.mcrel.org/toolkit/res/climate.asp

How to Shape Beliefs and Attitudes: http://www.principals partnership.com/AttitudeHandbookforUPWebs.htm

Tools for School Improvement Planning, from the Annenberg Institute for School Reform: http://www.annenberginstitute.org/tools/index.php

School Change Rubric, provided by Employers for Education Excellence an Oregon consortium of small schools: http://www.e3s mallschools.org/resources_program.html

O

Ownership Means
More than One

The basic principle which I believe has contributed more than any other to the building of our business as it is today, is the ownership of our company by the people employed in it.

James E. Casey, founder of UPS

Think About It

Do the members of your school community have an ownership stake in the school, or do they simply feel as though they are renting space?

Recommendations for school improvement over the last few decades have recognized the need for a broad definition of leadership. We also realize the need for those who are most closely involved in implementing programs and practices to be involved in decision making. There is a consensus among researchers about the importance of teacher participation in decision making as a way to improve efficiency and organizational effectiveness, even though there is no agreement on the level of participation.

Delegation of Responsibilities

One type of shared decision making is the delegation of decisions to assistants and other staff. Although this is a common management approach, if you want it to be effective, you must be sure that people know what is expected and desired of them, have access to the information needed, possess the technical knowledge needed, and have the interpersonal skills to accomplish the task.

Delegation is a useful strategy in two specific cases. First, when tasks are straightforward and the procedures are known, delegation is a way to increase your efficiency. Second, it is an effective method for personnel development when situations are more ambiguous. For example, a new assistant principal may benefit from chairing a major committee or being a member of a district work group.

Sample Delegated Responsibilities

Scheduling school facilities

Student discipline to an assistant principal

Personnel evaluation to an assistant principal

Processing work orders

Chairing school committees

Shared Decision Making

Shared decision making may include teachers collaborating with peers to address instructional issues, or it may include involving teachers in decisions about managerial concerns and school or district policy. There is no formula or perfect method for shared decision making; however, a common thread is the authentic nature of the involvement.

Examples of Teacher Involvement in Decision Making

Professional Development Committee: Teachers on the committee review applications from teachers to attend conferences and make recommendations and decisions about approved conference travel.

School Improvement Committee: Teachers and parents work with the principal to set school priorities, determine improvement projects, and allocate resources.

Principal's Advisory Committee: This group provides the principal with advice about important decisions. They serve as a sounding board for both day-to-day routines and important policy changes.

Scheduling Work Group: Many principals ask teachers, or department chairs in high schools, to work with them to determine the school's schedule and teacher assignments.

Budget Review Committee: Some principals share information about the school's budget with teachers and work with a small group to make decisions about spending priorities.

Benefits and Challenges

There are many benefits of shared decision making:

- Higher-quality decisions because more perspectives are considered
- Increased job satisfaction and morale
- Heightened sense of empowerment
- Greater ownership of school goals and priorities when participants have a stake in the decision
- Improved student achievement because of greater coordination of work among teachers

On the other hand, there are also challenges, or potential obstacles to shared decision making, which include the following:

- Expanded participation may require more time to make decisions
- Group dynamics may stifle ideas, leading to "groupthink"
- Polarization around points-of-view

- People feeling left out or that some have greater access and opportunity to influence decisions

Overall, the long-term benefits of shared decision making outweigh the mostly short-term, initial obstacles. When employees are active partners in critical decisions about the school, they have more ownership of the school's direction and a greater commitment to its success.

Planning for Shared Decision Making

The first step is to decide whom to involve. Ask yourself two questions.

1. Who is most closely involved?
2. How much people can contribute? What is their level of expertise?

You might also consider other factors in order to facilitate your decision. Hoy and Tarter (2008) have suggested that if people have a stake in the outcome and have some level of expertise, they should be involved. If people are indifferent to the outcome and have no expertise, no involvement is needed. Finally, if people are concerned with the outcome but lack expertise or have expertise but are indifferent, then they should have limited participation.

Things to Consider

- What is the task?
- Who has a stake in the decision?
- Who should appropriately be involved because of their expertise or their role?
- How will the group be organized?
- What are the group norms?
- How will the decision be made?
- What is the timeline for completion of the task?

Leadership Teams

One of the most common structures for shared decision making is a School Leadership Team, which may be called School Site Council or a School Improvement Team. It is generally composed of some combination of administrators, teachers, parents, school staff, and community members. Depending on your state or district, there may be laws or guidelines that determine the composition of your team. Some secondary schools (middle and high school) also include students.

As with any team, different points of view add value to the decision-making process. However, in order to be most effective, principals should provide three structures to the group:

Structures for Effective Leadership Teams

Establish norms of operation (how the group will function) and norms for decision making.

Be absolutely clear about the link to the school's mission and the importance of advancing institutional goals.

Develop and model thoughtful decision-making processes.

Depending on the specific needs of your school, you may have a variety of teams, such as instructional leadership teams or Principal's Advisory Councils. Your first decision is to determine what teams you need and how they will function within the overall decision-making structure.

Checklist for Formation of Shared Decision-Making Teams

_____	Is the purpose clear? Is the role well defined?
_____	Is membership representative? Is membership appropriate to the task?
_____	Are there agreed upon norms for operation? For decision making?
_____	Is there a mechanism to communicate with the larger school community? With other decision-making groups?
_____	What is the process for concluding the team's work?

You will want to be sure that the purpose of each team is clear and the role well defined.

Site-Based Management

The final type of shared decision making that we will discuss is site-based management, which is often used to describe local, school-level decision-making processes. Successful site-based management programs concentrate on improving student learning, have local autonomy, are characterized by a high level of involvement from stakeholders, have a clear alignment of vision and goals with school mission, make meaningful decisions, and reflect the prevalent culture of shared decision making.

As with any process of broad-based decision making, there are facilitators of effectiveness as well as obstacles.

Facilitators of Successful Shared Decision-Making Models	Barriers to Successful Shared Decision-Making Models
■ Appropriate, ongoing professional development for all stakeholders in the change process, including conflict management and decision-making models ■ Adequate time to meet, plan, implement, and evaluate decisions. Lots of time required initially to get started ■ Clear understanding of the areas/topics that the group can address ■ Communication plan to share information with stakeholders ■ Principal comfort and support ■ Accountability and responsibility of participants ■ Availability of technical assistance	■ Limits of decision-making authority are unclear and undefined ■ Principal directs and tells rather than guides ■ Only principal or superintendent held accountable for decisions ■ Groups do not have power to make "real" decisions and get mired in unimportant details

A Final Note

The job of a principal is too complex to isolate oneself when making decisions. The effective principal delegates some responsibilities but shares the decision-making process for some areas with stakeholders. There is an appropriate balance.

While ultimate responsibility for your school's program lies with you, it is important to remember that the evidence is clear—involving others in helping to make decisions results in "better" decisions and leads to greater commitment to the success of the school.

Skills for Principals

- Engage staff and community in a shared vision, mission, and goals for the school.
- Ensure that diverse stakeholders, even those with conflicting points of view, are involved in school decision making to build shared understanding and commitment to the vision and mission.
- Recognize the value of engaging staff and community in planning and implementing changes to school programs and activities.
- Model positive group processes that create a climate of openness and collaboration.

If You Would Like More Information . . .

Awakening the Sleeping Giant: Helping Teachers Develop as Leaders, by Marilyn Katzenmeyer and Gayle Moller (Corwin, 2001)

Improving Schools from Within: Teachers, Parents, and Principals Can Make the Difference, by Roland S. Barth (Jossey-Bass, 1990)

Lessons Learned: Shaping Relationships and the Culture of the Workplace, by Roland S. Barth (Corwin, 2003)

A research brief about decision making and how to determine who should be involved in a decision is available from the Principals' Partnership at http://www.principalspartnership.com/Decision MakingApr08.pdf

A research brief on site-based decision making is available from the Principals' Partnership: http://www.principalspartnership. com/sitebased.pdf

P

Professional Development Facilitates Growth

Learning is what most adults will do for a living in the 21st century.

Bob Perelman

Think About It

What types of professional development activities occur throughout the year in your school?

A key role of the principal is to recognize the importance of continued professional growth and development for the staff. It is critical that the principal model a commitment to continuous improvement and be an active participant in professional development activities

Traditionally, professional development focused on institutes, seminars, workshops, courses, conferences, and regional academies. Although those activities can support your professional development, contemporary professional development includes a wider variety of activities.

Contemporary Professional Development Activities

- Collegial support frameworks such as peer coaching and collaborative work teams
- Reflective inquiry frameworks such as study groups, critical friends, and action research
- Teacher leadership models such as lead-teacher and mentoring
- External support such as partnerships, networks and regional teacher centers

Contemporary Professional Development

According to the National Staff Development Council (NSDC, http://www.nsdc.org), contemporary professional development should have three defining characteristics:

1. Results driven
2. Standards based
3. Job embedded

In other words, professional development should follow a path that leads to clear results. Activities should be based on standards, and they should be thoroughly woven into the job rather than simply being an activity that is done as an "extra," possibly outside work hours or the work experience. Notice how these three elements drive a shift from our past focus on multiple activities to a cohesive plan.

Shifting from Traditional to Contemporary Professional Development

From . . .	To . . .
• Individual development	• Individual development and organizational development
• Fragmented, piecemeal improvement efforts	• Professional development driven by clear, coherent strategic plans
• District focused	• School focused
• Focused on adult needs and satisfaction	• Focused on student needs and learning outcomes
• Training conducted away from the job	• Multiple forms of job-embedded learning
• Transmission of knowledge and skills by "experts"	• Study by teachers of the teaching and learning process
• Staff developers who function as trainers	• Staff developers who provide consultation, planning and facilitation skills

The new model of professional development also views teachers differently. Older models, sometimes termed "in-service training," used a top-down approach. Activities were planned for teachers, who were the passive recipients of learning. The updated view sees teachers as active participants in their own learning.

It's helpful to consider this aspect of the shift in more detail. The new view thinks of teachers who have several needs as learners.

Needs of Teacher-Learners

- To be respected as intelligent, thoughtful, life-long learners
- To study individually, reflect, and then do
- To collaborate regularly with other teachers, especially in their specific content area(s)
- To share what they observe and experience
- To relate information to the real world of their classrooms
- To work with other teachers, both at their own site and other sites

Source: Adapted from National Staff Development Council.

Standards for Professional Development

The National Staff Development Council also provides a set of standards for professional development. This is a helpful tool as you plan your activities. Note that many states now have similar standards, usually modeled after these.

NSDC's Standards for Staff Development (Revised 2001)

Context Standards
Staff development that improves the learning of all students:

- Organizes adults into learning communities whose goals are aligned with those of the school and district (learning communities)
- Requires skillful school and district leaders who guide continuous instructional improvement (leadership)
- Requires resources to support adult learning and collaboration (resources)

Process Standards
Staff development that improves the learning of all students:

- Uses disaggregated student data to determine adult learning priorities, monitor progress, and help sustain continuous improvement (data driven)

- Uses multiple sources of information to guide improvement and demonstrate its impact (evaluation)
- Prepares educators to apply research to decision making (research based)
- Uses learning strategies appropriate to the intended goal (design)
- Applies knowledge about human learning and change (learning)
- Provides educators with the knowledge and skills to collaborate (collaboration)

Content Standards
Staff development that improves the learning of all students:

- Prepares educators to understand and appreciate all students, create safe, orderly and supportive learning environments, and hold high expectations for their academic achievement (equity)
- Deepens educators' content knowledge, provides them with research-based instructional strategies to assist students in meeting rigorous academic standards, and prepares them to use various types of classroom assessments appropriately (quality teaching)
- Provides educators with knowledge and skills to involve families and other stakeholders appropriately (family involvement)

Key Lessons from Award-Winning Schools

Based on our research with schools that have won the U.S. Department of Education's Award for Staff Development (Blackburn, 2000), we found seven key elements of effective staff development:

1. Clear purpose linked to research, student data, goals, and needs
2. Accountability through classroom use of ideas and impact on students
3. Development of a common, shared language
4. Shared decision making, which includes an emphasis on teacher input
5. Incorporation of relevant, practical, hands-on activities
6. Integration of opportunities for follow-up and application
7. Strong leadership and a positive, collegial atmosphere

First, you should have a clear purpose that is linked to research, student data, goals, and needs. Is there research to support what you plan? Is the planned initiative justified based on the data in terms of test scores, student surveys and feedback, or some other type of data? Does it align with the goals of your school? Finally, does it meet a need in your school?

The second key element is accountability in terms of classroom use and student results. Without accountability, you will likely not see a lasting impact. The first aspect of accountability is simple: How is the information learned actually used in the classroom? Interestingly, the teachers in the study were the strongest advocates of principals holding them accountable for classroom use.

For example, one teacher said, "My school allows me to go to conferences. However, when I came back no one held me accountable for what I had learned. If no one asks me what I learn and how I'm using it, then I'm not going to use it. Even the best ideas don't actually get translated into practice. When I come back from a conference I get hit with 500 other things." Next, consider student results. As an outcome of the planned professional development, what do you actually see in terms of the impact on students? Once again, although this can include test scores, you may also see an impact through increased student engagement, fewer discipline referrals, or an increase in the amount of homework completed.

The third key element is the development of a common shared language. When you use your professional development to develop a consistent frame of reference on a topic, it helps provide a focus for all stakeholders.

Fourth, if you want to increase the effectiveness of your professional development, create shared governance, which includes teacher input. This is more than just surveying teachers and asking them what they are interested in. Rather, create ways for teachers to be truly involved in the decision making that goes along with professional development. One school we worked with chose to implement a professional development committee that was in charge of the budget. As teachers began to decide how the money was allocated, the ownership increased.

The next key element is relevant and practical hands-on activities. Is the professional development relevant to the stakeholders? Does it have a practical value that is perceived by all participants? Are staff allowed to interact in ways that increase engagement? We want to create professional development activities that model best practices in the classroom.

The sixth element is follow-up. We know that if we plan a short, one-time activity, we will not see lasting results. How are you incorporating follow-up at every stage? What are the expectations for participants? Do you ask each teacher to complete an action plan? When we speak, we finish each session by asking participants to define one action they plan to complete when the return to their schools or classrooms.

Finally, strong leadership is crucial to any effective professional development. However, this is not just administrative leadership. This also includes teacher leadership. But without your leadership, your plan will fail. One principal we met provided an avenue for building teacher leadership for professional development in his school. Instead of having two regular faculty meetings each month, he used one for professional development for teachers. Teachers could share what they had learned at a conference, something they had read, or a new strategy they were implementing in their classroom. Although it took time, teachers became comfortable sharing their own practice, and they soon began asking for the second meeting.

Directly linked to leadership are the positive attitudinal elements in the school. How open are you, your administrators, and teachers to sharing learning? What is the willingness factor, the desire to collaboratively work together around a common goal? This truly reflects the culture of your school (see Chapter B: Beginnings, Endings, and School Culture) and is a direct result of your leadership in this area.

A Final Note

Contemporary professional development is a tool to effect change, to improve student learning, and to build collegial relationships. Moving from a traditional, scattered approach of isolated activities to a focus on coordinated strategies to support individual and collective change is the hallmark of effective professional development. Your modeling of active learning and engagement and facilitation of effective activities is critical.

Skills for Principals

- Support job-embedded, standards-based professional development focused on improving teaching and learning.
- Ensure that professional development addresses the need to meet the diverse learning needs of every student.
- Guide and monitor individual professional development plans.
- Focus school-based professional development activities on continuous improvement of teaching and learning.
- Provide support, time, and resources for teachers and other staff to engage in professional development activities.

If You Would Like More Information . . .

Evaluating Professional Development, by Thomas R. Guskey (Corwin, 2000)

Supporting and Sustaining Teachers' Professional Development: A Principal's Guide, by Marilyn Tallerico (Corwin, 2005)

Leading and Managing Continuing Professional Development: Developing People, Developing Schools, by Sara Bubb and Peter Earley (Paul Chapman,2007)

A set of professional development criteria: http://www.mcrel.org/PDF/ProfessionalDevelopment/6804TG_ProfDevelopCriteria.pdf

The National Staff Development Council offers the most comprehensive site of resources related to effective professional development (includes the national standards for professional development): http://www.nsdc.org/

$\mathcal{Q}$

Quality Teacher Evaluation

It takes humility to seek feedback. It takes wisdom to understand it, analyze it, and appropriately act on it.

Stephen R. Covey

Think About It

What is the purpose of teacher evaluation?

Another important facet of the principalship is teacher evaluation. Every school district has policies and procedures on the evaluation of teachers that are shaped by appropriate state law and local collective bargaining agreements. Teacher evaluation systems address the needs of two types of teachers—nontenured or probationary teachers and tenured faculty. Although specific requirements may differ, every state has a system of tenure for teachers. Similarly, the requirements for evaluating the performance of nontenured teachers are unique to each state.

Generally, nontenured teachers are evaluated every year while in probationary status. Most states require multiple observations, formative feedback to the teacher during the year, and a summative evaluation toward the end of the year. After receiving tenure, teachers may not be evaluated every school year. This can vary from district to district. The schedule of activities associated with the evaluation may be substantially different from that of a nontenured teacher.

Role of the Instructional Leader

There is no more important role for a principal than instructional leader. The principal is responsible for ensuring a strong instructional program at his or her school, but the principal is not the only person responsible for instructional leadership. Teachers deliver instruction and have expertise in curricular and instructional issues. The principal's role is to ensure a school climate that encourages collaborative work and is focused on providing every student with a high-quality educational experience.

Throughout this book, we have described tools that principals can use to foster such a climate. Chapter B describes the attributes of a positive school climate. Chapter I discusses instructional climate, and Chapters L and S provide tools for examining instructional practice.

Principals can do several things to ensure a school climate supportive of quality instruction:

- Communicate a clear vision for a high-quality instructional program
- Focus all school initiatives on improving teaching and learning
- Ensure an orderly, serious, and focused school setting
- Recognize the importance of collegial dialogue and discussion in improving instructional practice
- Provide support and obtain resources for instructional improvement
- Stay current on educational trends and developments and become knowledgeable about best practices
- Recognize and celebrate academic success to reinforce a school culture supportive of improved teaching and learning

Purposes of Evaluation

One of the challenges for principals is to balance the procedural requirements of local policy (number of observations, conferences, and written reports) with the desire to use an evaluation system that engages teachers in a reflective analysis of their teaching and promotes teacher growth.

In general, evaluation must be used as a tool to improve the performance of teachers. It should be guided by several beliefs.

Beliefs About Teacher Evaluation as a Tool for Improvement

- Provide specific feedback about areas for growth.
- Provide specific suggestions for ways to improve.
- Provide time and opportunity to improve performance.
- Provide resources (professional development, mentor, materials) to support growth.

Occasionally, growth does not happen. When that occurs, principals must be very attentive to the procedural deadlines in local district policies, state law, and the collective bargaining agreement. Failure to meet a deadline can result in the teacher continuing to teach for another year. Additional information about employment decisions may be found in Chapter F: Finding the Right People.

Evaluation is a procedural requirement embedded in state law and/or local policy and contractual language. It is important to follow all of the procedural requirements, but evaluating teacher performance also provides an opportunity to engage in conversations about teaching that allow teachers to think about their work and identify ways to continue to improve their teaching.

Teacher Practice

There are several descriptions of effective teacher practice. They include Hunter's direct instruction model (1982), Bloom's taxonomy, and, more recently, Danielson's (2007) four dimensions of teaching. The Danielson model has been used to revise many teacher evaluation systems.

The Danielson model includes four dimensions of teaching: (1) planning and preparation, (2) the classroom environment, (3) instruction, and (4) professional responsibility. The following table identifies some of the major characteristics of each dimension. A complete rubric is included in Danielson's *Enhancing Professional Practice* (2007).

Danielson's Four Teaching Dimensions

Planning and preparation	<ul><li>knowledge of content,</li><li>pedagogy,</li><li>resources,</li><li>instruction, and</li><li>assessment</li></ul>
Classroom environment	<ul><li>management of student behavior,</li><li>classroom space, and</li><li>classroom procedures and</li><li>creation of a classroom culture characterized by respect and rapport</li></ul>
Instruction	<ul><li>skill at communicating,</li><li>asking questions,</li><li>leading discussion,</li><li>engaging students in the lesson,</li><li>providing feedback, and</li><li>being flexible and responsive</li></ul>
Professional responsibility	<ul><li>committed to reflecting on their practice,</li><li>growing professionally,</li><li>communicating with families,</li><li>maintaining accurate records,</li><li>contributing to the school and district, and</li><li>being professional in their work</li></ul>

Source: Adapted from Danielson (2007).

Professional Learning and Teacher Growth

Teacher evaluation is a requirement in all states and districts. The periodic evaluation provides a snapshot look at teacher performance. These evaluations provide the basis for decisions about continued employment and the granting of tenure.

Principals are responsible for creating a climate in which professional learning and continued professional growth are central to the work of all teachers. Danielson and McGreal (2000) identified five factors that contribute to professional learning. They include opportunities for reflection on current practice, collaboration with other teachers and with administrators, opportunities for self-assessment and self-directed inquiry, the creation of a community of learners, and formative assessment.

Factor	Example
Reflection on practice	▪ Structured reflection as part of evaluation system ▪ Open-ended responses as part of assessment of all professional development activities
Collaboration	▪ Team, content, grade-level meetings focused on professional work ▪ Process for looking at student work
Self-assessment and self-directed inquiry	▪ Protocol for self-assessment of teaching practices ▪ Self-assessment component to supervision and evaluation procedures ▪ Identification of areas for professional study and growth
Community of learners	▪ Study groups ▪ Opportunity for peer observation ▪ Team, content, grade-level meetings ▪ Critical friends program
Formative Assessment	▪ Feedback that includes specific advice about strengthening practice ▪ Discussion about practice that is not judgmental but focused on professional growth

Each of these factors is influenced by the principal through the organization of the school—its schedule, planning time, and climate—openness to new ideas, an emphasis on professional dialogue and discussion, and a commitment to professional growth.

Glickman, Gordon, and Ross-Gordon (2004) suggest that effective supervision is characterized by six factors. Central to effective supervision is the recognition that teachers are adults and respond well to adult learning strategies. Teachers are also at different phases of their career, and their supervisory needs will vary. For example, there are vast differences between a novice teacher in his or her first year of teaching and a veteran teacher recognized for his or her skilled instructional capacities.

The Effective Supervisor . . .

- Understands that teachers are adults and respond well to the principles of adult learning
- Recognizes that all teachers are not at the same stage of their career and should not be treated alike
- Supports the needs of teachers at different stages of their career cycle
- Helps teachers to understand and learn from their teaching and from career events
- Accommodates the varied roles of teachers
- Considers the sociocultural context of the teaching
- Is empowering and motivating

Source: Adapted Glickman, Gordon, & Ross-Gordon (2004).

Formative or Summative

There are two types of teacher evaluations—formative and summative. Observations of teachers that are designed to provide feedback and to promote teacher growth are formative. When the principal must prepare a formal written document describing a teacher's performance, that is summative.

Conducting multiple observations of a teacher is always a good idea. Relying on a single observation or event as a source of data about teacher performance is inappropriate. Talking with the teacher about each observation and providing feedback about his or her teaching is part of the formative evaluation process.

Another way to think of it is that the formative process is designed to engage the teacher in a discussion and dialogue about his or her work, providing an opportunity for professional growth. The summative process is designed to check for results and measure a teacher's performance.

Supervision or Evaluation

Every year principals are expected to formally evaluate many of the teachers in their school. As mentioned earlier, state law or local policy will decide the exact process.

While some teachers may be formally evaluated, the principal should be supervising all teaching staff. Sally Zepeda described this work as "the most important work a supervisor does" (2007, p. 1). The role is to engage all teachers in a process in which they reflect on their teaching, collaborate with others, and grow professionally.

Instructional supervision is quite different from teacher evaluation. A timeline for observations and completion of evaluation documents usually guides an evaluation process. Supervision, on the other hand, is not a linear process.

Instructional supervision is intended to involve teachers in examining their own practices and, with support from colleagues and supervisor, strengthen and improve their practice.

Supervision vs Evaluation

Supervision		Evaluation
■ Supervisor, peers	Who	■ Administrator
■ Ongoing	Timing	■ Legal, contractual timelines
■ Improve learning, ■ teaching, ■ curriculum, and ■ classroom management ■ Focused on problem solving	Purpose	■ Quality control ■ Measurement of performance against identified standards
■ Derived from the teacher ■ Dialogue ■ Collaborative	Sources of data	■ Overt Identified in law or policy ■ Often negotiated
■ Focus on professional growth ■ Remains with the parties	Use of data	■ Evaluation form ■ Personnel file
■ Teacher ■ Focused on self-reflection and growth	Who makes judgment	■ Administrator
■ Collegial, look together at issues ■ Facilitative ■ Guide discussion	Role of observer	■ Line/staff relationship ■ Power and control

Three-Step Model

One of the most prominent models for promoting teacher growth is called the clinical supervision model. First suggested in the mid-1960s (Goldhammer, 1969; Cogan, 1973), most district requirements for teacher evaluation incorporate some variation of the approach. It is also a model frequently used to engage teachers in reflection on their teaching, a formative process.

The model is built around three components—a planning or pre-observation conference, observation, and a post-observation conference. The approach includes three phases: planning, observation, and analysis and reflection.

Clinical Supervision Model

Components	Phases
Pre-observation conference	Planning
Observation	Observation
Post-observation conference	Analysis and reflection

Planning or Pre-Observation Conference

During this step, the teacher and administrator meet to discuss the lesson being taught during the observation. It also provides an opportunity for the teacher to share any contextual information about prior instruction or about students in the class.

Conditions for Success

- Meet at a mutually agreed upon time and in a mutually agreed upon location.
- Presume positive intentions.
- Ask clarifying questions in order to understand the context (students, prior lessons, where this lesson fits into the curriculum) and the planned lesson.
- Arrange seating around a table or in way that promotes conversation; avoid sitting behind your desk.
- Avoid distractions—put all calls, pagers, or beepers on hold.
- Listen attentively and authentically.

Most important, the planning conference should include a conversation to identify the focus of the observation. Central to the clinical supervision model is the premise that the teacher can analyze and reflect on his or her own teaching. Part of that reflection is to identify the focus of the observation and to identify a tool the administrator will use to collect data about the lesson.

Discussion Prompts

- "Thank you for meeting today to talk about the upcoming visit to your class. In order to plan for that visit I would like to talk with you about your students, the lesson you plan, and ways in which I may be of help to you during the observation."
- "I always enjoy the opportunity to visit classrooms. What sort of data can I collect during my visit that would be helpful to you?"
- "Tell me about your students. What is important for me to know about them? Their learning?"
- "Talk with me about the curriculum for your class. What skills have you been working on? How is this lesson connected to prior learning?"

For example, one elementary teacher wanted data about the distribution of response opportunities among her students. The principal agreed to use a seating chart of the room to chart the number of times that the teacher called on or interacted with each student throughout the lesson. The result was a visual map of teacher–student interactions during the observation.

Key Steps of the Pre-Observation Conference

Decide the focus of the observation.

Determine the method and form of observation.

Set the time of the observation and post-observation conference.

Observation

Throughout the observation, the administrator gathers data about the focus area agreed to during the planning conference. You should be clear about the tool to be used to gather data. Your goal is for the teacher to be comfortable with the instrument used during the visit. Ideally, you have shared the form or tool with the teacher in advance of the observation. At the end of the observation, verify the meeting time and location for the post-observation conference, begin to analyze the data, and think about the questions that you will use during the conference to elicit teacher reflection and thinking about their lesson.

Key Steps of the Observation

- Conduct the observation.
- Verify the post-observation conference time and offer the teacher a copy of the data.
- Analyze the facts of the observation.
- Choose an approach to use during the post-observation conference.

Post-Observation Conference

The post-observation conference provides an opportunity for the administrator to meet with the teacher and have a conversation about the observation.

Conditions for Success

- Meet at a mutually agreed upon time and in a mutually agreed upon location.
- Presume positive intentions.
- Ask clarifying questions in order to understand the lesson and the teacher's thinking about both the design and the delivery of the lesson.
- Summarize and identify appropriate next steps.
- Arrange seating around a table or in way that promotes conversation; avoid sitting behind your desk.
- Avoid distractions—put all calls, pagers, or beepers on hold.
- Listen attentively and authentically; use paraphrasing to indicate that you are listening and understand what has been said.

This should provide an opportunity for the teacher to reflect on the data collected in the focus area and for the teacher to analyze and think about his or her teaching. The meeting should conclude with agreement on a plan to follow up and appropriate next steps.

Discussion Prompts

- "Thank you for meeting with me today. I would like to spend some time talking with you about the lesson."

- "Let's talk about your planning. When you plan a lesson, what are the things that you consider in its design?"

- "What strategies do you use to ensure that each lesson is linked to students' prior learning?"

- "Describe for me the ways you monitor whether or not your students are learning what you are teaching."

- "Talk me through the process you use to plan a lesson. What do you consider? How do you proceed?"

- "Occasionally, I'm in the middle of a lesson, and I know it is not working the way I would like. When that happens to you, how do you adjust your teaching? What data/information do you use to guide adjustments?"

- "When you teach this lesson again, what adjustments might you make in its design?"

- "Talk with me about the strengths of this lesson. What would you describe as its strengths? What evidence do you have to support these strengths?"

- "Let's spend a few minutes analyzing this lesson. How do you critique the lesson and its implementation?"

- "Let's think about next steps. What additional support can I provide for you and your teaching? What data can I collect? During my next visit, on what area of instruction would you like me to focus?"

- Note: This process should appropriately be modified for a less experienced teacher or one with performance concerns.

It is easy to shortcut this aspect of the process, particularly with stronger teachers, but it is a critical part of the reflective process and should receive its due attention. Often your most skilled teachers are most interested in an opportunity to reflect on their teaching and consider ways to continue to grow professionally.

Key Steps of the Post-Observation Conference

- Share the data and elicit the teacher's thinking about the lesson.
- Reflect on the teacher's comments so that you are clear on his or her thinking.
- Begin to think together about ways to refine the lesson. Focus on the things that should be affirmed and continued as well as things that might be modified.
- Problem solve through a discussion of the ideas and options.
- Agree on a plan and follow-up.

A Final Note

Teacher evaluation is another valuable tool for a principal. It allows you to focus on growth and models a continual need for reflection and improvement. Balance the procedural demands with a focus on collaborative analysis.

Skills for Principals

- Focus conversations with teachers on improving teaching and learning.
- Recognize the value of reflection to the professional growth of school personnel.
- Conduct personnel evaluations that enhance professional practice while following district and state policies.
- Utilizes a variety of strategies to lead people in examining deeply held assumptions and beliefs about teaching and learning.
- Model lifelong learning by continually deepening understanding and practice related to content standards, curricular requirements, instructional practice, assessment, and research-based best practices.

If You Would Like More Information . . .

Building Leadership Capacity in Schools, by Linda Lambert (Association for Supervision and Curriculum Development, 1998)

Supervision and Instructional Leadership: A Developmental Approach, by Carl D. Glickman, Stephen P. Gordon, and Jovita M. Ross-Gordon (Allyn & Bacon, 2004)

Helping Teachers Develop Through Classroom Observation, by Dian Montgomery (David Fulton, 2002)

Effective Teacher Evaluation: A Guide For Principals, by Kenneth D. Peterson and Catherine A. Peterson (Corwin, 2006)

Writing Meaningful Teacher Evaluations—Right Now! The Principal's Quick-Start Reference Guide, by Cornelius L. Barker and Claudette J. Searchwell (Corwin, 2004)

This research brief provides an overview of research on teacher evaluation: http://www.tqsource.org/publications/February2008 Brief.pdf

This short brief provides practical tips for teacher evaluations: http://www.principalspartnership.com/Teacherevaluation.pdf

R

Recognizing the Law

Good people do not need laws to tell them to act responsibly, while bad people will find a way around the laws.

Plato

Think About It

Which of these issues cause you the most concern: sexual harassment, religion, or privacy concerns?

Elsewhere in this book, we look at the legal implications for special classes of students (see Chapter X) and the legal aspects of student discipline (see Chapter E). But there are four other areas that can impact your job and consume your time if you violate the law.

1. Sexual harassment
2. Religion
3. Privacy
4. Students with disabilities

Sexual Harassment

Case law related to sexual harassment is one of the fastest growing areas of school law. The relevant law for most cases is Title IX of the Education Amendments of 1972. Under these rules, no individual may be discriminated against on the basis of sex in any educational program or activity receiving federal financial assistance, which includes virtually all public schools in the country.

School personnel must be aware of the legal requirements for preventing sexual harassment, whether the situation is student to student, adult to student, or adult to adult. There are two recognized types of sexual harassment: quid pro quo and hostile environment

Quid pro quo literally means to give something in exchange for something. In this scenario, there is an exchange, which most often involves sexual favors. Examples include a teacher exchanging a grade for some sexual favor or one student expecting a sexual favor from another student in exchange for providing protection at school.

The second kind of sexual harassment is called "hostile environment." A hostile environment may exist when conditions create a sexually charged atmosphere or when the work of one person is negatively affected because of the sexual tension present.

School personnel need to work to prevent sexual harassment because the U.S. Supreme Court has found that school personnel may be personally liable if they know about such harassment and fail to intervene to end it. In *Davis v. Monroe County Board of Education* (1999) the Court found that the deliberate indifference of teachers and administrators in an elementary school interfered with the educational opportunity of a female student when a male student repeatedly harassed her.

There are four key principles related to sexual harassment that must be considered:

1. It is gender neutral. The courts have found that in addition to harassing someone of the opposite gender, people can also harass members of the same gender.

2. Failure to act can result in personnel liability for school personnel.

3. It is important to provide "notice" to students, parents, and school personnel about sexual harassment, what to do if they experience it, who to talk with, and what they can expect from the school.

4. There is a requirement for action called an appropriate "standard of care."

There are also two relevant categories of sexual harassment with specific supporting case law. First, there is teacher-to-student sexual harassment. The Supreme Court found in *Franklin v. Gwinnett County Public Schools* that sexual harassment by a teacher constituted a form of discrimination and that monetary damages could be collected from the district. Principals must immediately act to investigate any alleged acts of sexual harassment. Failure to act can result in liability.

Next, there is peer sexual harassment, or student-to-student harassment. In this situation, the guiding case is *Davis v. Monroe County Board of Education,* in which a fifth-grade girl was sexually harassed by a male classmate. The girl and her parents complained to at least two teachers and the principal after the incidents. The lawsuit claimed that the school district had failed to act to prevent the harassment after being notified. This failure, in their view, created a hostile environment that inhibited the student's ability to learn. The Supreme Court ruled that when a school district acts with deliberate indifference to known acts of harassment in its programs and activities, that school district can be held monetarily liable.

In cases of alleged sexual harassment, there are two questions to consider:

1. Did school personnel act with deliberate indifference?
2. Was the harassment so severe that it barred the victim from access to an educational opportunity? (Did it interfere with his or her learning? Did it make him or her feel unsafe?)

As a principal, your first step is to set a positive example. Have a no-tolerance policy for behavior that may be offensive. Don't assume that everyone will interpret your words or actions the same way or that jokes or gestures are harmless or inoffensive. Remember, sexual harassment depends on how the person being harassed is affected, not on the harasser's intent.

Sexual harassment may be verbal, nonverbal, or physical, and sexual harassment is gender neutral. People of the same gender can sexually harass one another. Stay alert to the nonverbal cues of those in your school community.

Finally, investigate all complaints about sexual harassment. Never ignore sexual harassment, no matter how you personally feel about the situation. Throughout the process, be supportive of people who are being sexually harassed. Remember, your behavior sets the tone for your building.

Steps a School Can Take to Prevent Sexual Harassment

- Develop and publicize a sexual harassment policy that clearly states that sexual harassment will not be tolerated and explains what types of conduct are considered sexual harassment.
- Develop and publicize a specific grievance procedure for resolving complaints of sexual harassment.
- Develop methods to inform new administrators, teachers, guidance counselors, staff, and students of the school's sexual harassment policy and grievance procedure.
- Conduct periodic sexual harassment awareness training for all school staff, including administrators, teachers, and guidance counselors.
- Conduct periodic age-appropriate sexual harassment awareness training for students.
- Establish discussion groups for both male and female students in which students can talk about what sexual harassment is and how to respond to it in the school setting.
- Survey students to find out whether any sexual harassment is occurring at the school.
- Conduct periodic sexual harassment awareness training for parents of elementary and secondary students.
- Work with parents and students to develop and implement age-appropriate, effective measures for addressing sexual harassment.

Source: U.S. Office of Civil Rights.

Religion and the Schools

The second controversial issue is religion in the schools. According to the establishment clause of the First Amendment to the U.S. Constitution as interpreted by the Supreme Court in *Lemon V. Kurtzman* (1971), in order to be constitutional, a practice must have a secular purpose and must neither advance nor inhibit excessive governmental entanglement between government and religion.

Student Groups or Organizations

The Equal Access Act (EAA), passed by Congress in 1984 and upheld by the Supreme Court in 1990, created a requirement of access to school facilities for "non-curriculum-related" student groups outside the instructional day. This has been interpreted to mean activities held before and after school, during lunch, and during activity periods.

The EAA says that schools create a "limited public forum" when they allow non-curriculum-related groups to meet and use their facilities. A school that allows non-curriculum-related groups to meet under these circumstances cannot deny access or discriminate against groups based on religious, political, philosophical, or other speech content. Religious clubs or other religious student-led activities can only be prohibited if all other non-curriculum-based clubs are prohibited.

In 1993, the Supreme Court declared that religious speech was fully protected under the First Amendment and that school districts cannot engage in "viewpoint discrimination." This decision and others make it permissible to allow religious groups to rent and use public school facilities as long as those facilities are open to other groups wanting to hold meetings.

Prayer in Schools

School-sponsored prayer has been ruled unconstitutional by the Supreme Court in a series of cases. That includes prayers at the beginning of the day, before assemblies, and prior to sporting events. Public schools cannot be seen as endorsing a particular religious point of view. Schools must remain neutral on the issue of religion.

It is important to remember that the limits apply to activities that are conducted by the school. Individual students may continue to pray on their own and can talk about their personal religious beliefs. Occasionally, an individual student's right to practice his or her own religious beliefs may be limited if it infringes on other students' education by disrupting the school environment. For example, if a student wishes to proselytize about his or her beliefs during class, that might be considered disruptive and could be limited because it infringes on the ability of other students to learn.

Guidelines for Principals

According to the U.S. Department of Education, there are six specific actions that schools can take to provide an environment that is respectful of students' religious beliefs without being intolerant of different religious points of view.

School-Based Actions

The school's harassment policy should include protection from religious harassment.

Teachers and administrators should not support or participate in forms of student religious activities, including flagpole meetings or group prayer sessions.

Free speech is not an absolute right; the government can, to some degree, control the time, place, and manner of expression.

Schools may designate certain locations in the building for forms of student expression, including the distribution of literature.

Schools may teach about religion or its role in art, history, philosophy, music, and so forth.

Schools should include religion in their diversity statement to ensure that all religions and religious beliefs are given equal protection and recognition.

Student Privacy

The Family Educational Right to Privacy Act (FERPA) is designed to protect the privacy rights of students and their educational records. Under FERPA, "educational records" are those records, files, documents, and other materials that (1) contain information directly related to the student, and (2) are maintained by an educational agency or institution or by a person acting for such agency or institution. The major point is that educational records must be kept confidential.

Key Ideas from FERPA

- Parents have access to their child's educational records.
- Once students reach age 18, they control their records.
- A parent or eligible student can challenge content and request amendments.
- A parent or eligible student controls the distribution of records, including sending them to schools outside the current school district, but a district can send records if a parent or eligible student is notified.

> - Certain directory information can be released (name, address, date of birth, major, picture, degrees and awards) without parental consent, but certain types of information must be designated and parents provided a reasonable period of time to inform the agency that this information cannot be released.

There are some things that you as a principal can do to make sure your school complies with this law. First, talk with your teachers about the requirements of the law. For example, teachers should not post student grades with names. Second, make sure that the office staff who register students are familiar with the requirements and don't release any information without the required release. Finally, recognize that both biological parents have access to a student's records and may participate in teacher–parent conferences. Only with a court order barring the release of such information can you refuse to provide access to a noncustodial parent.

Students with Disabilities

Students with disabilities are guaranteed access to an appropriate educational program by several Supreme Court decisions and federal laws. The Individuals with Disabilities Educational Improvement Act (IDEA, 2004) is the prevailing federal law for students with disabilities in certain defined categories. Some of the law's protections include the following:

- Free and appropriate public education
- Least restrictive environment
- Related services such as transportation, health and nursing services, and psychological services
- Involvement of parents in all decisions about their child's program
- Development of an annual Individualized Education Plan (IEP) that describes the program of services for that specific child

Details about the IDEA may be obtained at http://idea.ed.gov/explore/home.

Discipline of Students with Disabilities

Principals can discipline students with disabilities if they follow the provisions of the child's Individualized Education Plan (IEP). If the student may be suspended from school for 10 days or less, no procedures beyond those provided other students are necessary. However, when suspension exceeds 10 cumulative days, it must be determined that the behavior leading to suspension was not a result of the child's disability. This is called a "manifestation determination hearing." If it is determined that the behavior and the disability are related, the IEP may be written to change the placement of the student.

Section 504

The Vocational Rehabilitation Act of 1973 is the other law that provides protections for students with disabilities. It provides for support and services to students who may not qualify under the IDEA but who have an identified disability. The specific services are not well defined in the law, and local policy often guides services to students.

Differences Between IDEA and Section 504

IDEA	Section 504
Student must qualify in one of 13 disability classifications	Three-part definition: Student must have (1) a physical or mental disability that (2) substantially limits (3) one or more "major life activities"
All students who are eligible under IDEA are also eligible under Section 504	Students can be eligible for Section 504 without being eligible for the specific protections of IDEA

A Final Note

Legal issues can consume major blocks of your time, particularly if you unintentionally violate the law. Understanding what is permissible within the law, then following the law, will streamline your job.

Skills for Principals

- Models personal and professional ethics, integrity, justice, and fairness and expect the same of others.
- Protect the rights and confidentiality of students and staff.
- Respect and follow the law.
- Behave in a trustworthy manner and use professional influence and authority to improve education and the common good.

If You Would Like More Information . . .

School Law and the Public Schools: A Practical Guide for Educational Leaders (4th ed.), by Nathan L Essex (Allyn & Bacon, 2008)

School Law: What Every Educator Should Know, A User-Friendly Guide, by David Schimmel, Louis Fischer, and Leslie R. Stellman (Allyn & Bacon, 2007)

School Law: Cases and Concepts (9th ed.), by Michael W. LaMorte (Allyn & Bacon, 2008)

The Clearinghouse on Educational Policy and Management, University of Oregon provides information on school law. Click on "School Law" under Trends and Issues: http://eric.uoregon.edu

The *American School Board Journal* includes a monthly column on a current legal issue: http://www.asbj.com

The *Education Week* School Law Blog provides up-to-date information about current legal issues affecting schools: http://blogs.edweek.org/edweek/school_law/

The U.S. Office of Civil Rights offers guidance about sexual harassment: http://www.ed.gov/about/offices/list/ocr/docs/sexhar01.html

5

Seeing with New Eyes

You can observe a lot just by watching.

Yogi Berra

Think About It

How much of your time is spent in classrooms observing what is happening? Is it limited to formal evaluations of teaching?

One concept that has grown in popularity in recent years is the "walk-through." Depending on the model, this can range from a structured, time-intensive approach to simply dropping in for a few minutes. However, in many cases, walk-throughs are often simply "wandering around" and not used appropriately.

The role of instructional leader requires that principals find ways to start and sustain conversations about student learning. One component of such change may be individual and collective reflection about current practice, and the instructional walk-through can be an effective tool to assist in the change.

We are not talking about a quick tour of the school or classroom but rather an opportunity to use classroom visits as a way to gather focused information about the educational experience of students. The purpose of the walk-through is to get a general sense of what is going on in classrooms, the use of instructional practices, and student learning.

There are several kinds of walk-throughs—some administrative, some collegial. The most valuable are those that are collegial and focus on gathering data about specific instructional practices. It is important to recognize that a short visit to any classroom provides only one snapshot of the instructional program and should not be used for any form of evaluation.

Don't skip over that point. Any short visit does not provide a full picture of the classroom. We spoke with an administrator who explained why he disliked walk-throughs.

> When I was a teacher, my principal at the time was a fan of short walk-throughs. She visited my room for three minutes. Although I was teaching a grade-level lesson in my science room, she stepped in while I was reviewing some basic knowledge in response to a question from a student. During the faculty meeting that afternoon, she used my classroom as an example of poor teaching. She said I wasn't teaching on grade level skills, despite the fact that my test scores were the highest in the school. Any effective walk-through should take into account the context of the situation. At a minimum, a principal should ask questions to understand what is happening.

A misuse of walk-throughs can undermine your efforts to build a collegial atmosphere and can destroy the trust of your faculty. However, effective walk-throughs can help you build progress toward goals.

Types of Instructional Walk-Throughs

The walk-through was developed by the Institute for Learning at the University of Pittsburgh (under director Lauren Resnick). As the institute states, "A walk-through can be varied to serve different educational needs. All walk-throughs are organized to improve learning and instruction, but differing relationships among the persons participating in the Walk-through and their specific purposes for participating define the need for different Walk-through modes."

We will discuss several types of walk-throughs. Data collected during walk-throughs can be used with faculty to examine instructional practice, to look at the balance between student-centered and teacher-directed learning, and to provide information about the implementation of new initiatives. Each situation is different. Understanding the different types of walk-throughs will help you decide which one(s) will be most effective in your situation.

Five Types of Walk-Throughs

1. Observational walk-throughs

2. Collegial walk-throughs

3. Supervisory walk-throughs

4. Administrative walk-throughs

5. Focused walk-throughs

Note: The first three types were developed by the Institute for Learning.

Observational walk-throughs are conducted by the school principal and a person(s) from outside the district's environment. The purpose is to identify the presence of key indicators of learning. For the outside observer, one challenge is to have a clear understanding of what to look for, including specific indicators. For both observers, the goal is to identify the presence of the indicators as they look at student work and talk with students and their teachers.

The second type is the *collegial walk-through.* It is similar to an observational walk-through in that an outside person(s) is involved, but the role is different. In this model, each observer is someone who is viewed as a colleague of the principal or other school leader. The focus of this walk-through is different. In this case, the goal is to gather evidence on how key principles are used to engage students in learning the essential content. After the walk-through, the participants discuss recommended professional development or other experiences or resources that would improve their teaching.

Next, *supervisory walk-throughs* may involve a principal and his or her immediate supervisor. The purpose is to analyze teaching and learning, with an eye toward evidence of student work as well as strategies that enable students' learning of the content. According to the Institute for Learning, "the focus of discussion is on progress made since the last Walk-through visit and the best type(s) of professional development to meet teachers' needs, so that learning and instruction show continuing improvement."

The fourth and fifth types were developed by teachers and administrators, and each incorporates ideas from the first three types. *Administrative walk-throughs* are conducted by the administrative staff of the school and are designed for administrators to gather information about the instructional program. They may be conducted by the building administrative team and provide data about the school's operation. *Focused walk-throughs* are conducted by teams of teachers and others they invite. The goal is to gather data about the learning and instruction process around targeted areas of improvement. Most often, members of the school's School Improvement Team organize the walk-through and facilitate use of the data.

Student-Focused Walk-Throughs

Goldberg (2008) suggests that another way to use walk-throughs is to focus on student learning rather than on teaching. He suggests that this approach may reduce teacher anxiety. This may be helpful because other researchers have found that principals shy away from providing negative feedback, particularly to vocal or defensive teachers.

In this approach, the principal asks questions rather than making statements about teacher performance. Instead of making assumptions, the principal gathers data by asking questions of the teacher.

Sample Guide Based on Goldberg's Questions

Guiding Questions	Teacher's Response
What were the goals of the lesson?	
To what extent did students achieve these goals?	
Did all students achieve the goals?	
What should I know about the students in your class and their learning?	
What might you change the next time you teach this lesson?	
Summary point(s):	

The questions are designed to focus the teacher on student learning rather than his or her own performance. The intent is for the teacher to reflect on the lesson, how it was delivered, and whether it met student needs. The purpose is not for the principal to analyze or evaluate the teacher's performance.

A superintendent in New Mexico asked students three questions when visiting classrooms:

1. What are you doing?
2. How are you doing with it?
3. Why are you doing it?

The superintendent said that the answers told a lot about the students' experience. The answers provided insights into what the students understood. In this district, these three questions turned into the building blocks for classroom instruction, as teachers used them to incorporate student reflection and self-assessment in lessons.

Three-Minute Walk-Through

Downey and colleagues (2004) have suggested another approach for a walk-through. They suggested a tightly organized three-minute model focused on teacher decision making and not focused on teacher practice. This model is designed to be brief, to promote teacher growth rather than evaluation, and to promote reflective conversation and coaching.

They identified five components for the walk-through—student orientation to work, decisions about curricular objectives, instructional practices, evidence of prior curricular and instructional decisions, and health and safety issues.

Student orientation to work	• Are students on task? • Are they focused on the lesson? • Are they paying attention to the teacher?
Decisions about curriculum	• What were the objectives of the lesson? • Were they aligned with district and state standards?
Decisions about instruction	• What instructional practices were used in the classroom? • Did they engage students in the lesson?

Prior curricular and instructional decisions	• What indication is there of prior curricular and instructional decision making? • What evidence of student learning?
Health and safety issues	• How safe was the classroom? • Did you recognize any health and safety concerns?

Source: Adapted from Downey, et al. (2004).

Sample Applications of Walk-Throughs

A Los Angeles school of nearly 4,000 students used instructional walk-throughs as part of its school improvement process. Each month, the school leadership team identified an instructional focus based on *Classroom Instructional Strategies That Work* (Marzano, Pickering, & Pollock, 2001).

Monthly Instructional Focus: Summarizing and Note Taking

Specific Indicators	Classroom Examples
Summarizing: Students are provided opportunities to verbally summarize chunks of information, either with a partner or small group.	
Summarizing: Students are provided opportunities to summarize information in writing.	
Summarizing: Students demonstrate a thorough understanding of summarizing, which means "substituting, deleting, and keeping some things and having an awareness of the basic structure of the information presented."	
Summarizing: Other information observed.	

Note taking: There is a clear format for note taking that students have been taught and that they use consistently.	
Note taking: Students are required or encouraged to take notes and are given time for review and revision of notes.	
Note taking: Students are encouraged to use notes as an effective study guide for tests.	
Note taking: Other information observed	
Strengths observed related to summarizing:	
Strengths observed related to note taking:	
Questions or areas for possible improvement:	

Teams of teachers conducted the walk-through, charted their observations, and posted the information on large chart paper in a central location. Faculty meetings were used for content-area teachers to meet, review the data, and develop explicit plans for improving instruction in the focus area.

As you can see from the following sample, a simple chart can help you collect data. For standard information, such as grade level, subject, class level, and/or groupings, use a checklist format for quick collection of data. Then provide ample space for information you gather that is more open ended. Again, you will need to adapt the categories and demographic data to match your situation.

Sample Instructional Focus Walk-Through Form:
Marzano's Nine Strategies

Grade Level	Subject	Class Level	Grouping(s)
___Six ___Seven ___Eight ___Mixed	___Math ___LA ___Science ___Social studies ___Related arts (specify:) ___Other (specify:)	___Mixed abilities ___Honors/GT ___Special needs	___Whole class ___Small groups ___Pairs ___Individual

Strategy	Evidence
1. Identifying similarities and differences	
2. Summarizing and note taking	
3. Reinforcing effort and providing recognition	
4. Homework and practice	
5. Nonlinguistic representations	
6. Cooperative learning	
7. Setting objectives and providing feedback	
8. Generating and testing hypotheses	
9. Cues, questions, and advance organizers	

Strongest evidence of strategy use:
Questions to ask about incorporation of strategies:

Because most walk-throughs are just a few minutes, it is likely that everything on your chart may not be seen in every instance. The data should provide a set of "snapshots" of instructional practice in your school. It should not be used to evaluate or assess the instructional effectiveness of staff.

A Final Note

No matter which type of walk-through you choose to utilize or adapt, the focus should always be on gathering data that can be examined for patterns. The patterns bring together useful information about the need for large-scale change, as opposed to providing in-depth information about one teacher's classrooms. The data are then used to inform instructional improvement. A focus on growth will yield results.

Skills for Principals

- Supervise instruction as the first priority.
- Develop an assessment and accountability system to monitor student progress.
- Develop the instructional and leadership capacity of the staff.
- Maximize the time spent on quality instruction.
- Provide effective guidance toward a rigorous curriculum, quality instructional program, and accountability system.

If You Would Like More Information . . .

The Instructional Leaders' Guide to Informal Classroom Observations (2nd ed.), by Sally J. Zepeda (Eye On Education, 2008)

The Three-Minute Classroom Walk-Through: Changing School Supervisory Practice One Teacher at a Time, by Carolyn J. Downey , Betty E. Steffy , Fenwick W. English, Larry E. Frase, and William K. Poston (Corwin, 2004)

This article addresses teachers' walk-throughs: http://www.education world.com/a_admin/admin/admin494.shtml

These articles from *Education World* describe practical experiences with walk-throughs:

http://www.educationworld.com/a_admin/columnists/hall/hall006. shtml, http://www.educationworld.com/a_admin/admin/admin 480.shtml

T

Teaming with Families and Community

The ability to relate and to connect, sometimes in an odd and yet striking fashion, lies at the very heart of any creative use of the mind, no matter in what field or discipline.

George J. Seidel

Think About It

As you think about the families of your students and the larger school community, how closely are they involved in the life of your school?

As a principal, you likely spend a portion of your time working with parents and other family members of your students. Too often, much of that time is negative, coming after a major discipline problem or crisis. Another critical part of your job is leading a coordinated schoolwide effort to interact with families in ways that support students, families, the school, and the larger community.

Every student in your building has a family and comes from a community, both of which influence the student. And teachers and administrators interact with families and the community every day—sometimes in direct ways, sometimes indirectly. Even if you do not live in the same community as your students, every family in that community likely knows who you are as the principal of the school. Recently, in a high-poverty school, we noticed that the curriculum coordinator made several contacts with parents during a trip to the local grocery store. Parent involvement is more than a monthly meeting at the school; it is the sum of all your interactions with parents and family members of your students.

Intuitively, we know that involving parents and family members in a partnership has a positive impact on our students. When parents are involved both at home and at school, students do better in school and stay in school longer. When a parent and teacher work together to help a student in a specific subject area, such as reading, students typically improve in that area. Students do best when their parents play four key roles related to their child's learning: teacher, supporter, advocate, and decision maker.

There are also benefits for teachers. Teachers who involve parents have a more positive attitude about families and stereotype them less. There is growing evidence that well-designed programs and practices that incorporate the school, family, and community benefit students, families, and schools.

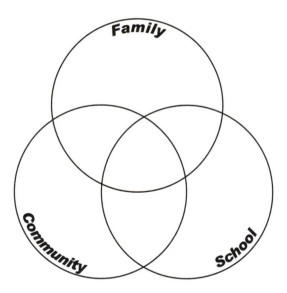

Time is a common roadblock to coordinated parent/family involvement. But a related issue is lack of knowledge or training. Few teachers or administrators are prepared to work with families and communities as partners in their children's education. However, if you are willing to make the time to talk with the families in your school and listen to their needs, then you have taken the first step to building an effective partnership.

How to Respond

It's important to remember that, just as you balance the common needs of all your students with specific, individual attention, you will need to do the same with the families in your school. The four strategies that follow are applicable to all the families in your school, but you will need to customize specific activities within each strategy to best meet the needs of particular families or groups of families.

Strategy 1: Communicate, Communicate, Communicate

First, establish a variety of clear communication procedures, some in print, some in person, and some electronic. Keep in mind your family populations. Technology can be a wonderful tool for communication, but everyone may not have ready access. Or, some families simply may not be as comfortable communicating through technology; they may prefer a more personal connection. By communicating in multiple and varied ways, you can meet the needs of all of your families.

Publish a family-friendly school newsletter on a regular, consistent basis. Be sure to share necessary information about the school, but also include topics of interest to parents. Be sensitive to the diversity in your community. Do you need to publish a version in a different language? The same holds true for other procedures. Print signs in your building in the languages spoken by school families. Do you need to establish bilingual hotlines and help lines? If you have a large percentage of families who do not speak English as their native language, provide language training so that you and your teachers can communicate on a basic level with the family members.

Involve families in a variety of activities throughout the year. You might start with an orientation to the school, but it's important to provide ongoing activities that help you communicate with groups of family members. Providing transportation, food, and child care will boost attendance, especially for those who may not be able to attend otherwise. It's also important to consider the scheduling, perhaps offering the meetings at a variety of times to accommodate parents' work schedules.

Topics for Family Activities

The Basics of Your New School

Homework? Here's How to Help!

What Does It Mean? How to Understand Your Child's Test Scores

Overwhelmed by College Applications? What You Need to Know

You are likely to have new students who enter your school after the start of the year. Create a welcome wagon to greet new families and help them with the transition to a new school. Enlist other families to deliver a "Welcome to Our School" packet of key information that includes a personal note from you and other school personnel.

Finally, parents value a personal connection with the teacher and others in the school who work with their son or daughter, so encourage communication from all school personnel. Promote the use of personal notes, e-mails, and phone calls to build a strong connection with families.

Vernisa Bodison, as a new assistant principal, wrote personal notes to her sixth-grade students, welcoming them to middle school. In addition to receiving responses from the students, she began building a personal relationship with each of them. Students and parents noticed, and she started the year on a firm foundation for success.

Strategy 2: Create and Support Authentic, Meaningful Roles

Next, be sure that you create and support roles for family members that are authentic and meaningful. As we mentioned in the last section, rather than simply holding a meeting, provide activities that include training and support. Maintain a vibrant school/family/teacher organization that actively seeks to involve all families in the group.

Also, provide ways for families to participate in meaningful decision-making roles. You will find that the different perspectives can add depth to your discussions, and family members will appreciate that you value their input. If you are attempting to implement a change in your school, their support will also be critical.

Another alternative is to craft volunteer opportunities that capitalize on family members' expertise, abilities, and interests. Be creative as you develop options that add to the typical volunteer activities found in most schools.

Volunteer Opportunities

Be a guest speaker for classes

Record audio versions of text materials to use with at-risk readers

Co-sponsor interest clubs

Create brochures and other marketing materials

Help with specific classroom projects

Strategy 3: Provide Support and Resources

It is also important to provide support and resources for the families of your students, although the specific types will vary depending on your specific population. Therefore, you must first understand your families and then match your resources to their needs.

One possibility is to create a family and community learning center. Find a physical space with adult-sized furnishings; then add basic refreshments and information helpful to parents. As you create a library of materials they can access, don't forget to have material that is written in appropriate language. You may need information written in a different language, such as Spanish, but you also may need to simplify the educational jargon in materials, realizing that your audience may not understand complicated terms.

Possible Resource Materials

Information about free or inexpensive medical and dental resources, including immunizations

Locations of libraries and local museums

Brochures about the importance of balanced nutrition in student meals

Public transportation schedules

Books about child growth and development

Brochures on parenting workshops

Child care providers

Parent support groups

Community mental health facilities

Another alternative is to create family support groups that deal with topics identified by parents and family members. You can then make the learning center available to these and other groups for meetings.

Finally, publicize what you are offering. Mention the resources in newsletters and other communications. Provide clear, inviting, noticeable directional signs. Keep some of the resource materials in the main office, with a note that more are available in the resource center. You can build a terrific center for families, but if no one uses it, you have wasted your time. Make sure those who need it the most know it exists.

Strategy 4: Support the Larger Community

Fourth, seek ways to move beyond the doors of your school and support the larger community. You might identify opportunities for students to participate in community service activities. Or, choose to celebrate the cultures of your community with specific school programs. Collaborate with other agencies or groups in the area to create a framework for delivery of services, such as immunization clinics or dental and medical services. For example, an inner-city school in Jackson, Mississippi, partnered with local doctors to provide a free health screening day for all parents in the community. The only requirement was that they bring their school-age child with them. Parents received hundreds of dollars of services, the students participated in fun activities, and the bonds between the school, families, and community were strengthened tremendously.

A Final Note

Connecting with families can be time-consuming, but it is a priority that is critical to the long-term success of your school. Remember, you both have the same priority: the well-being and learning of the students in your school.

Skills for Principals

- Value the participation and contributions of families and the school community in ensuring school success.
- Promote understanding and appreciation of the school community's diverse cultural, social, and intellectual resources.
- Build positive relationships with families and caregivers.
- Ensure that school programs, policies, and practices support the critical role of families and caregivers in the educational success of students.
- Advocate for children, families, and caregivers within the school and in the larger school community.
- Build and sustain effective community partnerships that support the success of students.

If You Would Like More Information . . .

School, Family, and Community Partnerships: Preparing Educators and Improving Schools, by Joyce L. Epstein (Westview Press, 2001)

Making Your School Family Friendly, by Steven M. Constantino (National Association of Secondary School Principals, 2003)

Developing Successful Parent Partnership Programs, by J. L. Epstein and N. Jansorn, *Principal–Connecting with Families,* 2004: http://www.naesp.org/ContentLoad.do?contentId=1121

"Connecting Schools, Families and Community," from e-Lead, offers description of community building standards and resources for principals: http://www.e-lead.org/principles/connection.asp

This site gives an example of family and community engagement policy from Memphis City Schools: http://www.mcsk12.net/admin/Parental-Involvement/Family-Engagement-Policy.pdf

U

Under Pressure:
School Safety

Plans are nothing; planning is everything.

Dwight Eisenhower

Think About It

What are your plans for dealing with a crisis?

School safety is an area that should never be taken for granted. In the best-case scenario, you have plans that ensure the safety and well-being of all students and faculty, and your school structures provide a secure climate. In the safest schools, there are contingency plans for every possibility, including crisis situations.

As a principal, your role is to provide leadership to ensure safety in all aspects of school life. Note our wording—provide leadership. With all of your responsibilities, you cannot plan every detail. To be an effective leader, it's important to share decision making with other stakeholders.

160

The Foundation

Begin by creating a School Safety Council. In addition to providing recommendations and making decisions, members of the council can assist with training of faculty and staff.

Suggested Representatives to the School Safety Council

Principal (chair)

School faculty/staff

Students (where appropriate)

Parents

Community representatives

Medical personnel

Law enforcement representatives

First responders

Your School Safety Council will be an important support structure as you assess your current status and make ongoing adjustments in three key areas of school safety: planning, climate, and access.

Safety Plans

First, assess your plans in all areas of safety.

Types of Information

Identification procedures

School/classroom access procedures

Evacuation routes

Emergency plan

Safety drill information

Emergency contact numbers

Inclement weather plans

System of school crime tracking, reporting, and feedback

> Discipline/anti-bullying policies
>
> Locations of emergency equipment
>
> List of first responders
>
> Science lab procedures

Next, make the needed modifications or create plans in areas without specific procedures. Finally, be sure appropriate people know pertinent details, such as training options, emergency contacts, and evacuation plans. Information should be shared verbally, in writing through the provision of safety manuals, and visually through posters.

Safe and Caring Climate

Safety should be an integral part of your overall school climate. What is your vision for the climate in your school? (see Chapter B: Beginnings, Endings, and School Culture). It's likely that you want every student and/or faculty member to feel safe and secure, which includes feeling valued and cared for. Critical components in this area include discipline policies, anti-bullying and violence prevention activities, and advocacy strategies.

Discipline

Schools should have a clear discipline code of student behavior and conduct that encourages respect of others (see Chapter E: Effective School and Classroom Discipline). As with all our recommendations, it's important to gather input from all stakeholders so as to ensure ownership. Teachers and other staff members should strive to be impartial, consistently rewarding appropriate behavior and sanctioning unacceptable actions.

Anti-Bullying/Violence Prevention

As a part of schoolwide discipline policies regarding respect for others, it is important to reinforce a stance against bullying behaviors, including racial or sexual harassment (see Chapter R: Recognizing the Law). Appropriate actions include addressing student discipline issues in a firm manner that does not shame students, implementing peer mediation programs, and instituting a no-tolerance policy.

Advocacy

One of the best strategies for minimizing problems, or keeping initial discipline problems from growing into larger issues, is to ensure that students have a personal relationship or connection with a caring adult. For example, in middle or high school, organize an advisory program that provides an opportunity for every child to have a personal connection with an adult.

There are many types of advisory or advocacy programs. You want to work with your teachers to determine the organization and function of a program in your school.

Access

In this area, think of yourself as a gatekeeper. From this perspective, you must determine who has access to your school as well as the level of access for the variety of people in your school. This includes screening potential employees, developing policies about volunteers and guests (see chart), having a system for those who enter the building both during the day and outside school hours, and having a policy for use of the building for nonschool activities.

Sample Guidelines for Volunteers and Visitors

- Complete any required legal requirements, including background check and/or fingerprinting.
- Attend orientation meeting, if appropriate.
- Follow all procedures for signing into and out of the building; maintain a log of name, time of arrival, time of departure, purpose of visit, and person visiting.
- Wear a name tag when in the school.

Of course, all school-based procedures should be aligned with district policies, and local, state, and federal laws. Additional areas for consideration include identification cards, a safe and secure entranceway, and traffic and parking procedures.

Dealing with a Crisis

Prepare and Prevent

As we've already discussed, the best way to deal with a crisis is to prevent one from occurring. This happens when you plan and prepare for every possibility and put structures in place that prevent or at least minimize a crisis. You can have a comprehensive plan, appropriate structures, and it's still not enough. That's when you need to respond.

Also be sure and conduct practice drills. Students and staff need to know procedures and be comfortable that they will work when you need to use them.

Respond and Recover

When a crisis happens, first, take a deep breath. Identify the type of crisis and determine the needed response. Implement your plan and communicate appropriately with all parties. It's particularly important that you have a plan for communicating with families and the media (see Chapter K: Keys to Public Relations). Have a system for letting providing families with accurate, up-to-date information about the event. Once the crisis has passed, it's not over; you need to help everyone recover and return to a normal learning environment as soon as possible. There is no formula for knowing how to balance attending to the emotional needs of students, teachers, and parents while shifting the focus to learning. But even an outward return to instruction is healthy and helps everyone move forward. During the process, identify appropriate follow-up interventions, and monitor to see whether or how much additional support is needed. You may need to call in extra help or specialized personnel. In an area private K–12 school, when a ninth-grader was killed in a car accident at the beginning of the year, administrators quickly enlisted the assistance of middle school teachers to help counsel students, as they had stronger relationships with the ninth-graders.

Next, without waiting too long, discuss the lessons learned and make needed adjustments to your plans. As President Dwight Eisenhower pointed out, it is the planning, not the plans, that makes a difference. It may be painful, but taking time to analyze and reflect on the process is an important step to help you plan for the future. Finally, create ways to commemorate the event. Some people may want to simply forget, but others need to find a positive response or way to remember.

A Final Note

Ultimately, school safety is an area of your job in which you invest tremendous energy and time in covering every contingency, all the time hoping you never need to use the crisis portion of the plan. You will see the benefits of your planning if and when you face a crisis.

Skills for Principals

- Monitor and evaluate management and operational systems that deal with the welfare and safety of students and employees.
- Understand the requirements for a school safety or crisis management plan.
- Prepare and plan for implementation of school crisis management plans.
- Create and sustain a positive relationship with police and other emergency responders.
- Protect the welfare and safety of students and employees.
- Nurture and sustain a culture of collaboration and trust.

If You Would Like More Information . . .

Making Your School Safe: Strategies to Protect Children and Promote Learning, by John Devine and Jonathan Cohen (Teachers College Press, 2007)

Racist Incidents and Bullying in Schools: How to Prevent Them and How to Respond When They Happen, by Robin Richardson and Berenice Miles (Trentham, 2008)

Violence in American Schools: A New Perspective, edited by Delbert S. Elliott, Beatrix A. Hamburg, and Kirk R. Williams (Cambridge University Press, 1998)

University of Oregon: Clearinghouse for Educational Policy and Management. Offers links to more than 30 sites covering issues of school safety: http://www.eric.uoregon.edu/trends_issues/safety/links.html

School Safety Resources: Emergency Plan Development, compiled by
JUSTNET: Justice Technology Information Network:
http://www.nlectc.org/assistance/ssres_emergencyplan.html

A series of three feature articles on school safety is available from the
Principals' Partnership archives: http://www.principalspartner
ship.com

This article contains questions and tips to consider about school safety:
http://securitysolutions.com/news/school-security-tips/?cid=
most-popular

Vision

A vision is not just a picture of what could be; it is an appeal to our better selves, a call to become something more

Rosabeth Moss Kanter

Think About It

What is your vision for your school? How many others in your school community share the same vision?

Holding a clear sense of vision or purpose for a school is important for the principal. Not only must you have a personal vision, but also you must be committed to working collaboratively with teachers, staff, teachers, and students to articulate a clear and compelling vision for the school. In this chapter, we will look at how to create a personal vision statement, how to build a shared vision statement for your school, and ideas for using that vision as a motivational tool.

Creating a Personal Vision Statement

There is an old saying, "You have to take care of yourself before you can take care of others." The same is true of vision. Before you can help others build a shared vision, you must have a vision of your own. Writing a statement of personal vision provides three benefits:

1. Helps to clarify values and beliefs
2. Identifies priorities in your life
3. Clarifies what is most important and how you want to spend your time

The purpose of a vision statement is to inspire, energize, and motivate. It should be emotional and reflect your feelings. Using the following process, you can create your own statement of personal vision. Be sure to include sensory details to provide power to your statement. Also, the more time you invest in reflection at the beginning of the process, the clearer your finished product will be.

Ethics and Integrity

Principals must act ethically and with integrity. As you develop your personal vision, it is important to consider your own personal ethic. Joan Shapiro and Jacqueline Stefkovich (2005) found that individuals view their work through a variety of quite different lenses. They described these "ethics" as the ethic of justice, ethic of care, ethic of critique, and the ethic of the profession.

Your personal ethic consists of the most fundamental beliefs you hold about life, about your work, and about relationships with people. As you develop your personal vision, filter it through your personal ethic. Consider whether it reflects your most deeply held beliefs about your life and work.

Process for Developing a Personal Vision Statement

Step 1: Think about your personal and professional life. Describe what you would like to achieve and the contributions you would like to make. Think of it as something already accomplished. Describe what it looks like and feels like. For example, imagine hovering in a hot air balloon over your life. Imagine your life as successful as it might be—what would you see, what would you feel, what would you hear?

Step 2: Consider the following things based on what you have written—self-image, relationships, personal interests, and community. Examine each item in your draft to ensure that it still fits.

Step 3: Develop a list of values. Identify the most important values in your life. Once this is done, review the list and rank them from most to least important. Remove the least important. Re-rank if appropriate. Check for relevance with your earlier statement. Eliminate any item that is not relevant.

Step 4: Use the items from the first three steps to develop a statement about who you are. Review and edit the statement as often as needed until you believe that it accurately reflects who you are.

Creating a Schoolwide Vision

The North Central Regional Educational Laboratory identified a "clear, strong and collectively held vision and institutional mission" as one of the six critical components of an effective school. A mission or vision statement is the shared vision of people in a school about their ultimate purpose. In other words, it is a collective commitment of the school community.

Effective mission statements are short and easily remembered; they are used for setting goals and priorities for the school, teachers, and students; and they are helpful in selecting the specific programs, resources, activities, and personnel used to achieve the goals. As you consider the development of a mission statement (or the revision of a current mission statement that may not be effective), incorporate the characteristics of effective statements.

Components of a Mission or Vision Statement

- A statement of purpose: Overall purpose for the school
- An indication of uniqueness: What distinguishes the school from others
- An explicit statement of commitment: Above all else, what is most important
- A clear value position: Reflection of the school's core and fundamental values, values that will guide individual behavior and school practice

Now that you have an understanding of the purpose and components of a mission statement, let's look at the process for developing an institutional mission statement. If you currently have a mission statement, you may want to adapt this process to review your current statement. Even the best mission statements need periodic review and revision. This review process allows your school staff to adjust the mission based on current information and needs. It also allows staff to recommit to the school's core values and beliefs.

Process for Developing an Institutional Mission Statement

Activity 1: What are the things that people are pleased with and frustrated with at this school? (Designed to get the issues on the table.)

Activity 2: As we begin planning for our future, what values are most important to you as we create our vision statement? (Use of "I believe" statements focus on the important things.)

Note: A helpful approach is to have the group read some common things. For example, information about the developmental needs of students, future trends, and information about recommendations for schools at that level. Often professional associations (National Association of Secondary School Principals, National Association of Elementary School Principals, National Middle School Association, Association for Supervision and Curriculum Development) have useful resources. Shared readings create a common base of information and are particularly useful to minimize the barriers between teachers and parents when parents often defer to teachers as the "experts."

Activity 3: Imagine it is the year 2012. We have been able to operationalize our beliefs. What will we see? What will we her? What will our school feel like? Describe the vision. (Helps to identify the target the school will work toward.)

Activity 4: In work groups, develop a draft mission statement to be shared with the larger group. (Development of multiple models promotes discussion, clarification, and consensus building.)

Once you have developed a draft statement, move to the next phase to prepare a completed statement.

Moving from Statement to Implementation

Step 1	Task
Share draft with constituent groups to elicit feedback.	Distribute draft statement to constituent groups and provide opportunity for critique and feedback.

Strategies
<ul><li>Distribute to staff using e-mail; include open-ended questions to provide feedback.</li><li>Include draft in parent mailing with response sheet for feedback (perhaps e-mail option).</li><li>Provide an opportunity for members of the writing group to present the draft at a staff meeting and lead table discussions about the draft.</li><li>Hold an after-school or before-school session at which teachers can meet with the writing team members to discuss the draft.</li></ul>

Step 2	Task
Revise the statement based on feedback.	Writing group meets and reviews feedback and makes revisions.

Strategies
<ul><li>Hold a half-day meeting to review feedback and make revisions.</li><li>Meet after school to review feedback and make revisions.</li></ul>

Step 3	Task
Seek agreement from appropriate constituent groups.	The revised statement is shared with constituent groups and their agreement and support is sought.

Strategies
<ul><li>Share with the Building Leadership Team and seek their support.</li><li>Share with the faculty and seek their support.</li><li>Share with parents and ask the parent–teacher organization for support.</li></ul>

Step 4	Task
Finalize the mission statement.	Make any needed adjustments, if any.
Strategies	

- Share the statement widely with all school constituent groups.
- Post the statement in every classroom.
- Add the statement to school letterhead.
- Include the statement on the school Web site.
- Create a banner displaying the statement and hang it in the entrance to the school, in the gymnasium, or in a multipurpose room.

Vision as a Motivational Tool

Vision is one of the most effective tools for personal and group motivation. Having a vision, then revisiting that vision regularly, helps you and your faculty focus on what is most important and balance the competing demands you face.

In *Classroom Motivation from A to Z*, Barbara recommended that teachers write vision letters. The task is to imagine that it is the last day of school. Write a letter or e-mail message to another teacher describing the past year: all that students accomplished, how they have changed, and what they have learned. It is a simple activity designed to keep teachers motivated, but it can serve as a building block for your vision process.

Ask your teachers to write the letter to you. It is the last day of school, and this past year was the best year of their teaching careers. What happened in their classroom? What happened in the school? How did their students change? How did they grow personally and professionally? Then, use the letters as a part of a discussion with each teacher about their vision and how it relates to yours and the vision for the school. It's a meaningful way to start the conversation about vision in your school.

Gather Data and Assess Your Progress

You will also want to routinely gather data (see Chapter D: Data Are the Focus) about your school. Use the data with your School Improvement Team or other group to discuss progress toward achieving your school's vision. Use these discussions to modify and refine the vision if appropriate.

A Final Note

The job of a principal begins with vision. If you don't have a vision, then you won't have a clear direction when the pressures mount. Take the time to develop your own vision and to build a shared vision among your school community.

Skills for Principals

- Develop a shared vision of high performance for every student.
- Mobilize staff to achieve the school's vision.
- Use varied sources of information to shape a vision, mission, and goals for the school.
- Aligns the school vision, mission, and goals with district, state, and federal policies.
- Incorporates a variety of perspectives into development of the school vision, mission, and goals.
- Craft a consensus about the vision, mission, and goals of the school.
- Advocate a vision of learning in which every student has equitable, appropriate, and effective learning opportunities to achieve at a high level.

If You Would Like More Information . . .

Leaders with Vision: The Quest for School Renewal, by Robert J. Starratt (Corwin, 1995)

Lead, Follow, or Get Out of the Way: How to Be a More Effective Leader in Today's Schools (2nd ed.). by Robert D. Ramsey (Corwin, 2006)

Visionary Leadership in Schools: Successful Strategies for Developing and Implementing an Educational Vision, by Edward W. Chance (Charles C. Thomas, 1992)

This article provides suggestions for building a collective vision: http://www.ncrel.org/sdrs/areas/issues/educatrs/leadrshp/le100.htm

This article provides a step-by-step guide for developing a personal vision statement: http://www.timethoughts.com/goal setting/vision-statements.htm

This newsletter describes information about leadership vision: http://www.itstime.com/aug2006.htm

W

Working Together
for the Future

Coming together is a beginning. Keeping together is progress. Working together is success.

Henry Ford

Think About It

Is your school a learning community? What does that term mean to you?

The term "learning community" has become commonplace in the conversation about school reform. You can hear it used to mean almost any sort of collaborative work, including working with community personnel to improve schools or extending classroom practice into the community.

The professional community of learners suggested by Astuto and colleagues (1993) describes a school in which teachers and administration continuously seek and share learning and then act on what they learn. The goal is to improve effectiveness focused on improving the learning of students. A professional learning community is a powerful professional development tool and a potent strategy for school change and reform.

175

Benefits of Professional Learning Communities

The earliest discussion of factors that impact teacher work was conducted by Rosenholtz (1989), who found that teachers who felt supported in their own ongoing learning and instructional improvement were more committed and effective than those who did not receive such support. Support such as expanded professional roles, cooperation among colleagues, and participation in teacher networks led to a high sense of efficacy. Teachers with a high sense of efficacy were more likely to adopt new classroom behaviors and more likely to remain in the profession.

Benefits for Staff

Reduced isolation of teachers

Increased commitment to mission and goals of the school

Collective responsibility for students' success

More likely to be professionally renewed

Higher satisfaction, higher morale, lower rates of absenteeism

Commitment to making significant and lasting changes

Greater likelihood of undertaking systemic change

Learning that defines good teaching and classroom practice

Creates new knowledge and beliefs about teaching and learners

Source: Hord (1997).

McLaughlin and Talbert (1993) confirmed these findings and suggested that teachers who had opportunities for collaborative inquiry and the learning related to it were able to develop and share their learning. The ultimate benefit of a professional learning community is a positive impact on learning for everyone—including students.

Benefits for Students

Lower absenteeism

Greater academic gains than in traditional schools

Smaller achievement gaps between students from different backgrounds

Decreased dropout rate

Increased learning distributed more equitably in smaller high schools

Source: Hord (1997).

Characteristics of Professional Learning Communities

As we stated earlier, the idea of a learning community is used to describe a wide range of activities. Richard DuFour (http://www.bpe.org/documents/DuFour-WhatarePLCs.pdf) says the "the term has been used so ubiquitously that it is in danger of losing all meaning." As we have discussed throughout this book, communicating effectively with all stakeholders to build and share your vision is critical so that everyone has a similar focus. There are six building blocks to an effective professional learning community.

Building Blocks

- Shared mission and values: Developed from a staff's commitment to students' learning
- Collective inquiry about school issues: Application to solutions that address students' needs
- Supportive and shared leadership: Power and authority shared through inviting staff input in decision making
- Action oriented and comfortable trying new things: Openness to feedback, collection and analysis of data to guide adoption of new initiatives
- Focused on continuous improvement: Recognize the value of routine examination of practice and making changes when appropriate
- Results orientation: Clarity about outcomes and "laser light" focus on achieving the desired results

Source: Adapted from Hord (1997) and DuFour and Eaker (1998).

Overall, effective learning communities have three defining characteristics:

1. Assurance of student learning
2. Culture of collaboration
3. Focus on results (whatever it takes)

Who Thrives in a Professional Learning Community?

Although there is clear research as to the benefits of professional learning communities, some teachers and administrators resist the idea. Those who function best in this environment tend to be intellectually curious, analytical, critical thinkers, creative, reflective readers and listeners, stimulated by new ideas, and adept at "reconstructing" knowledge. That does not mean teachers or administrators who do not have those characteristics cannot be effective in a professional learning community; however, they may need more time and support to thrive (see Chapter N: New Challenges, New Opportunities).

Role of the Principal in a Professional Learning Community

The school change literature clearly recognizes the role and influence of the principal on whether change will occur in a school (see Chapter Y: Year After Year: Sustaining Success). Transforming a school into a professional learning community can be done only with the sanction and support of the leader. Therefore, the decision to move to a professional learning community ultimately lies with you.

In order to build a successful learning community, you must abandon the traditional position of authority and participate in your own professional development. Your role is that of a learner, along with teachers and other staff, "questioning, investigating, and seeking solutions for school improvement" (Hord, 1997). In order to set aside the traditional hierarchy and recognize there is a need for everyone to contribute, you must be skillful at facilitating the work of staff. As you respect the process of inquiry to promote understanding and construct mutually agreed upon solutions, you will need to participate without dominating.

Shifting the Role of the Principal in a Professional Learning Community

Move from . . .	Toward . . .
Decision maker	Participant in the learning process
Expert	Learner
Director	Facilitator
Dominating leader	Participating leader

Structures of a Professional Learning Community

There are structures you can use to facilitate an effective professional learning community. First, build schedules and organizational structures that reduce isolation (see Chapter M: Managing Schedules for more information). Identify time when teachers can work collaboratively in grade-level or content teams. Locate a room where teams can meet and engage in substantive conversations about school goals and student learning. Some schools locate classrooms to promote conversation between grade levels and content areas. For example, one wing of a middle school we worked with included math, science, language arts, and social studies teachers who taught common students.

Next, incorporate policies that encourage greater autonomy, foster collaboration, and enhance effective communication. The staff in one elementary school where we worked agreed that every grade-level policy would be shared with teachers in the prior grade as well as the next grade so that consideration could be given to its impact on those grades. Staff found that this useful to the design of more broadly accepted policies.

Third, provide time for staff development within the regular school day (See Chapter P: Professional Development). Fourth, work with your faculty and staff to develop a willingness to accept feedback and work toward improvement. When hiring, look for the same characteristics in prospective candidates. Fifth, be open to sharing professional practice. Be transparent about your own learning, and encourage all those around you to do the same. Finally, create an atmosphere of trust and respect among colleagues. Nothing undermines a professional learning community more than a lack of trust and respect.

A Final Note

Professional learning communities can transform the culture of your school. They provide benefits to teachers, students, and the entire community. Building a professional learning community takes time and a change in leadership style, but the results are worth it.

Skills for Principals

- Find the time and resources to build a professional culture of openness and collaboration, engaging teachers in sharing information, analyzing outcomes, and planning improvement.
- Model openness to change and collaboration to improve practices and student outcomes.
- Collaborate with staff, families and caregivers, and the community to develop a shared vision, mission, and goals for the school.
- Use and analyze varied sources of information about current school practices to shape the vision, mission, and goals of the school.
- Engage stakeholders, including those with conflicting points of view, in shaping the vision, mission, and goals of the school.
- Develop shared commitments and responsibilities that are distributed among staff and community for achieving the vision, mission, and goals of the school.
- Guide and support job-embedded, standards-based professional development focused on improving teaching and learning.

If You Would Like More Information . . .

Professional Learning Communities: Communities of Continuous Inquiry and Improvement, by Shirley M. Hord (Southwest Educational Development Laboratory, 1997)

Professional Learning Communities at Work: Best Practices for Enhancing Student Achievement, by Richard DuFour and Robert Eaker (Solution Tree, 1988)

Learning by Doing: A Handbook for Professional Learning Communities at Work, by Richard DuFour, Rebecca DuFour, and Thomas Many (Solution Tree, 2006)

Redesigning Schools for Success: Implementing Small Learning Communities and Teacher Collaboration, by Charles, E. Ruebling (Center for School Redesign, 2006)

These articles provide information about learning communities:
http://www.sedl.org/change/issues/issues61.html,
http://www.learningpolicycenter.org/data/briefs/LPC%20Brief_J
une%202008_Final.pdf,
http://pdonline.ascd.org/pd_online/secondary_reading/el
200405_dufour.html

The X Factor:
Special Populations
in Your School

*Ignorance of the law excuses no man: Not that all men know the law,
but because 'tis an excuse every man will plead, and no man can tell
how to refute him.*

John Selden

Think About It

How many different subgroups or special populations make up your
student body?

Every school contains a number of special populations—students who
require extra support or attention. Addressing the needs of students who
qualify for special education services is the most obvious group, but there are
many others, some more visible than others. These groups of students often
have legal protections. In this chapter, we will discuss many of the special
populations found in schools and describe the legal requirements for
meeting their needs.

Basic Legal Concepts

Both federal law and many states laws provide protection for groups of students. Those groups are called "classes," which are groups of students who share a demographic characteristic. Generally, the laws and subsequent court decisions say that any protected class cannot be disproportionately affected by a school policy, program, or practice. For example, any program that limits accessibility for students in one of the protected classes would not be permitted. The Fourteenth Amendment to the U.S. Constitution declares that no state shall deny any person within its jurisdiction equal protection of the laws. Because school districts are subdivisions of the state, the amendment is applicable to the district and schools within the district.

Special Populations or Classes of Students

Race

Linguistic minorities

Immigration status

Homeless status

Gender

Handicapping condition

Race

Race is one of the protected classes. Title VI of the Civil Rights Act of 1964 bars discrimination on the basis of race, color, or national origin for organizations receiving federal financial assistance, which includes virtually all school districts. The Equal Educational Opportunities Act of 1974 guarantees public school students equal educational opportunity without regard to race, color, sex, or national origin. The key point: School programs, policies, and services cannot discriminate against students based on race, color, or national origin.

English as a Second Language— Linguistic Minorities

Another one of the protected classes is a student who does not speak English. The case *Lau v. Nichols* (1974) affirmed their right to receive educational services. Their rights are protected by the Fourteenth Amendment and Title VI of the Civil Rights Act of 1964. The U.S. Supreme Court decided that there is no requirement to provide instruction in the student's native language.

Immigration Status

Students who are not legal immigrants are also protected. In *Plyler v. Doe* (1982), the Supreme Court found that they are protected by the Constitution's Fourteenth Amendment and that schools cannot deny enrollment based on immigration status.

Homeless Status

The McKinney-Vento Homeless Education Assistance Improvement Act (2001) protects students who are homeless. School districts must enroll such students and cannot have programs that "stigmatize or segregate students based on homeless status." Homeless students must also be provided transportation to and from school.

Gender

Because gender is one of the protected classes, a school's programs, policies, and practices cannot discriminate based on gender. Title IX of the Civil Rights Act of 1972 is often thought of as applying to athletic opportunities, but it has much broader applications. For example, it also relates to single-gender schools and classrooms, to school clubs and activities, and to individual classes available to students. The Fourteenth Amendment also provides due process protections for students when gender discrimination is an issue. In Chapter R: Recognizing the Law, we discuss the ramifications of Title IX in terms of sexual harassment.

Title IX of the Civil Rights Act of 1972 prohibits gender discrimination in institutions receiving federal financial assistance. It permits the separation of students by gender on sports teams within contact sports.

The Pregnancy Discrimination Act of 1978 also protects female students from discrimination based on pregnancy status. Schools may offer alternative programs for pregnant students, but they cannot compel attendance in those programs by pregnant students.

In 2007, the U.S. Department of Education revised its rules on single-gender schools and single-gender classes. They are permissible, but schools must ensure that every student, regardless of gender, has access to comparable programs. For example, if a school district has a single-gender program in math and science, there must be a program for both males and females.

Handicapping Condition

The key legislation related to handicapping conditions is the Individuals with Disabilities Education Improvement Act (IDEA, 2004). This federal law requires states receiving federal educational funds to provide educational services to students with specific disabilities. The law requires that parents must be active partners and must agree to all testing and placement of students. Individual states develop their own rules and regulations for implementing the federal law.

Key Ideas of IDEA

- Handicapped students are entitled to a free and appropriate public education. That means that schools must provide programs that meet their needs at no cost to the family.

- Individualized Education Plans (IEP) are required for all handicapped students. That means that each qualifying student must have an education plan that addresses his or her individual educational needs. Schools cannot limit options to programs that are currently offered, nor can schools place students into programs that are not identified in their IEP. Parents are part of the process of identifying educational plans and must agree to the plan.

- Students must be placed in the least restrictive environment. There is no legal requirement that students be placed in inclusive settings. However, students cannot be placed in self-contained classrooms when an inclusive setting would better meet their needs.

- Students stay in their current setting or placement until an agreement is reached in a new IEP for placement in a new setting. This is called the "stay-put" requirement.

- Handicapped students are entitled to related services such as transportation, social work, or occupational therapy if they are identified in their IEP.

A related law, the Vocational Rehabilitation Act of 1973, Section 504, provides for the needs of students who require educational support because of an identified handicapping condition. It does not have the same requirements as IDEA for identification and service to students. Because the law is not very explicit, local districts develop their own plans. The key idea is that schools must accommodate students with handicaps that affect their education. For example, a student might need to sit close to the front of the room or might need to have additional time to complete assignments.

Finally, the Americans with Disabilities Act (1990) has ramifications for schools. This federal law requires that physical facilities cannot limit the educational services available to students. Therefore, schools are required to ensure that all of their facilities are handicap accessible.

A Final Note

Special classes of students add to the flavor of a school. However challenging it appears, meeting their specific needs is a legal requirement. A basic understanding of the law as it relates to each group will ensure that you adequately provide for each group.

Skills for Principals

- Ensure the academic and social success of every student.
- Promote understanding and appreciation of the community's diverse cultural, social, and intellectual resources.
- Build and sustain positive relationships with families and caregivers.
- Advocate for children, families, and caregivers.
- Seek out and collaborate with community programs serving students with special needs.
- Link to and collaborate with community agencies for health, social, and other services for families and students.

If You Would Like More Information . . .

Administering Special Education Programs: A Practical Guide for School Leaders, by H. Roberta Weaver, Mary F. Landers, Thomas M. Stephens, and Ellis A. Joseph (Praeger, 2003)

The School Leader's Guide to Student Learning Supports: New Directions for Addressing Barriers to Learning, by Howard S. Adelman and Linda Taylor (Corwin, 2006)

Wrightslaw: Special Education Law (2nd ed.), by Peter W. D. Wright and Pamela Darr Wright (Harbor House Law Press, 2007)

Effective Schooling for English Language Learners: What Elementary Principals Should Know and Do, by Patricia Smiley and Trudy Salsberry (Eye On Education, 2007)

Teachers of English to Speakers of Other Languages, Inc.: http://www.tesol.org/s_tesol/index.asp

This article provides tips for providing accommodations for students with disabilities (geared for high school): http://www.nasponline.org/resources/principals/ Academic%20Accomodations%20for%20Students %20With%20Disabilties.pdf

These articles provide information on dealing with homeless students: http://www.wested.org/pub/docs/431, http://www.nasponline.org/resources/principals/ nassp_homeless.aspx

Y

Year After Year: Sustaining Success

People often say that motivation doesn't last. Well, neither does bathing—that's why we recommend it daily.

Zig Ziglar

Think About It

How many new initiatives are implemented in your school each year? Which ones have lasted over time?

School communities are under increasing pressure to dramatically improve the educational experience of students. Principals are faced with the need to lead their staff and community in examining current practice, implementing changes, and sustaining them from year to year.

Ron recently visited with a Tucson high school principal to discuss the challenges she faced at her school. When she became principal of her school, she found that lots of improvement projects were under way, but almost all were the responsibility of an individual department or program. There was no unifying theme and no uniform purpose. She described it as "lots of good people trying to do things that made a difference," but there was little coordination among the projects. Across the campus, there was a lot of distrust, cynicism, and no interest in talking about the issues.

At her first staff meeting, the principal invited staff to write down their concerns, fears, and frustrations on index cards. The cards were collected and the principal placed them in a large paper bag. She shared her vision for making this school high performing and invited the staff to join her on a journey to transform their school.

"I also told them that they could return to their rooms and go about preparing for the start of the school year or they could join me in the courtyard at noon for a ceremonial burning of the cards." Less than one-third of the staff met in the courtyard to observe the cards representing their frustrations, concerns, and fears going up in smoke.

Those who attended became members of a newly constituted School Improvement Committee. The committee developed specific plans to improve literacy and mathematics instruction at the school and to create a safe learning environment for all students. The principal worked with those who did not attend to encourage their participation but also supported and assisted their efforts to transfer if so desired.

Three years later, the high school is one of the highest performing in the district. Student achievement is vastly improved. Far fewer students drop out each year. It has one of the highest percentages of students taking advanced placement classes among district high schools.

Mary Clark, principal of Conway Middle School, begins her school year in a similar manner. She gives her teachers an "Invitation to a Fresh Start." Teachers write down anything that is holding them back from a fresh start to the new year, and then they hold a celebratory event throwing all of the slips in a trash can. As she says to them, "Remember to treat yourself well, then release yourself from the past!"

Today, you are cordially invited to a Fresh Start!

Take the time to jot down thoughts, feelings, or ideas that in the past have kept you (or are currently keeping you) from enjoying your work and/or performing to the best of your ability.

Treat yourself—release yourself!

Dynamics of the Change Process

In order to make changes that are long lasting, we must first consider the change process. According to the North Central Regional Educational Laboratory, there are six key components that characterize successful school improvement initiatives:

1. A clear, strong and collectively held educational vision and institutional mission
2. A strong, committed professional community
3. A focus on learning environments that promote high standards for student achievement
4. Sustained professional development to improve learning
5. Successful partnerships with parents and community organizations and agencies building a broad base of support
6. A systematic planning and implementation process

We discuss each of these elsewhere in this book. In Chapter V, we address vision. Chapter O includes information on building a strong professional community, which is also a part of Chapter P, along with sustained professional development. Additionally, Chapter W describes professional learning communities. Chapter I provides information on focused learning environments, while Chapter T describes partnerships with parents and the community. Finally, Chapter N and W include information about working with others to plan and implement change.

However, it is important to consider them in the context of sustaining growth. Most school improvement projects last more than one year and require a long-term commitment to success.

Central to all sustained improvement efforts is the presence of a clear, mutually agreed to and collectively supported vision statement. It serves as the litmus test for all improvement efforts. For example, does this activity align with our vision and support our agreed upon mission?

Because school improvement is a long-term process it is important to provide continued professional development for those expected to implement the changes. There is a lot of evidence that the most important professional development comes after an initiative has begun. Often, it is only then that teachers and others fully understand the implications of the project. They have appropriate questions about implementation and support.

Finally, rarely do school improvement projects achieve everything they set out to achieve. Not only is it important to involve teachers and other school constituents in planning, but also it is important to involve them in monitoring implementation and helping to make any adjustments that might be needed. For example, the pace of implementation might require modification or additional professional development might be useful.

Stages for Launching an Initiative

Next, in order to build a strong foundation for change, allow time to work through a series of stages. The Oregon Small Schools Initiative (http://www.e3smallschools.org) identified six stages for the launch of any initiative:

1. **Study**: Time devoted to examining and learning about an issue and associated reforms. School, district, and community members can examine current practices and programs, identify gaps in student learning, and discuss how the reform can improve the educational experience of students.

2. **Stage**: During this component, a school reviews its current programs, practices, and policies and creates a shared vision for the future. Including a diverse group of people in this process helps to support nurture and sustain the change.

3. **Design**: This step involves the creation of standards or design frameworks that will be used to develop the specific program.

4. **Build**: During this part of the change process, the specific program components are developed and linked to the school's improvement plan.

5. **Launch**: Implementation of the plan involves mobilizing human and financial resources . It includes the provision of professional development to support the change.

6. **Sustain**: Monitoring implementation and building capacity to sustain the initiative after its launch characterizes this stage. Also included is gathering and analyzing data about the impact of the change.

At one middle school that Ron worked with in suburban Chicago, there was interest in redesigning the program to provide more time for some subjects and to ensure that the program provided students with the knowledge and skills for success as they moved to high school and beyond.

A person knowledgeable in middle school programs was asked to visit the district; review the current program; talk with students, teachers, and parents; and then make recommendations to the district.

As a result of this review, the district decided to launch a school improvement project that would involve teachers and parents in reviewing the program and making recommendations to strengthen offerings.

The first step was to involve teachers and parents in the development of a school mission statement. They used the process outlined in Chapter V: Vision. Several committees were convened to study specific issues such as curricular offerings, exploratory classes, enrichment opportunities, teaming arrangements, and ensuring positive relationships. Each group read about the topic, reviewed research, and talked about the school's students. Each group developed recommendations that, when implemented, would change the school's program.

To monitor implementation, a Steering Committee of teachers and parents was organized. This committee was asked to review all recommendations and ensure that they were aligned with the school's mission. They also created an implementation timeline and determined which recommendations would be the first to be implemented. They were also responsible for monitoring the implementation to ensure its long-term success.

Tapping into Motivation for Support

Finally, as we point out in Chapter N: New Ideas, New Challenges, in order to build a broad base of support for a change, you must consider the motivational factors of your stakeholders.

Two Motivational Questions

1. What is the value of the change?
2. Can I be successful with the change?

Value

There are two specific steps you can take to help all stakeholders see the value of the innovation. First, in order to help each person see the value of the proposed change, *be sure to provide a clear, compelling rationale.* Unless provided with a compelling rationale for changing programs and practices, school communities resist change. As a part of the conversation, use data that are clear, meaningful, and linked to student success (see Chapter D). Next, *provide ample opportunities for staff, students, and parents to be appropriately involved* in planning reform initiatives. Such participation should include known supporters as well as known dissenters, in order to build a cadre of people who understand the issue and can advocate for recommended changes.

At one school in central Ohio, the principal organized a work group of teachers and family members to work on assessing their program. The school had a history of underachievement among several subgroups of students. Their first task was to discuss and agree on the measures that they would use to measure the success of their program. The list of indicators they developed included the normal things—test results, attendance, and demographic information, among others.

The group was then asked to review the information and identify patterns or trends that they observed. This review led to a recognition that many students were not doing well in school.

Rather than simply announce the agenda, the principal built value and support for examining current practices by taking the time to involve teachers and families in identifying the problem.

Success

There are also two key building blocks that will help stakeholders succeed. First, *identify specific indicators of success*. During the initial planning stage, prior to launching any initiative, be sure to identify how you will measure success. Be as specific as possible to give all stakeholders a vision of how they will be successful. Then, after initiating the change, routinely collect data about both implementation and the impact of student learning. Use the data to guide decisions about sustaining the initiative.

Second, *provide support for implementation*. Once a reform is launched, it is important to support implementation with professional development linked directly to the initiative. It is also critical to provide time for those involved to routinely meet debrief and make appropriate adjustments.

Four Ways to Ensure Long-Lasting Change

Value	Success
Provide a clear, compelling rationale. Provide appropriate opportunities for stakeholders during the planning process.	Provide support for implementation. Identify specific indicators of success.

Middle schools in one district in western New York were under-achieving. To address the issue, a planning committee was organized consisting of teachers, administrators, and parents from each school. Their first task was to develop an agreed upon statement of vision and mission for the middle school program. Before developing the statement, they gathered and reviewed data about local demographic trends, social and economic factors affecting schools, current data about the schools, and information about effective practices.

This review led to a shared commitment for change—to create a middle school program that would prepare students for success as they moved to high school and beyond. This shared commitment provided the clear rationale to support changes to the educational program.

The planning committee then made recommendations to continue some school programs, to modify others, and to implement some new approaches. The committee was involved in developing a plan for implementing each recommendation and measuring its success.

A Final Note

Although we have provided a series of steps and building blocks designed for long-lasting change, please note the underlying thread of broad-based ownership throughout the information. The most effective way to ensure success over the years is to develop a broad foundation of support. The enemy of sustained changed is a "Lone Ranger" mentality. If you are the owner of the initiatives, they die as soon as your attention is directed elsewhere. Throughout the change process, build shared ownership (see Chapter O), and you'll see long-lasting results.

Skills for Principals

- Establish, conduct, and evaluate processes to engage staff and community in implementing and sustaining the school's vision, mission, and goals.

- Develop shared commitments from staff and community to nurture and sustain the school's vision, mission, and goals.

- Engage diverse stakeholders, including those with varied points of view, in the implementation of the school's vision, mission, and goals.

- Advocate with staff and community for the resources (time, people, money) to nurture and sustain the school's vision, mission, and goals.

If You Would Like More Information . . .

From At Risk to Academic Excellence: What Successful Leaders Do, by Franklin P. Schargel, Tony Thacker, and John S. Bell (Eye On Education, 2007)

School Leadership that Works: From Research to Results, by Robert J. Marzano, Timothy Waters, and Brian A. McNulty (Association for Supervision and Curriculum Development, 2005)

Leading in a Culture of Change, by Michael Fullan (Jossey-Bass, 2001)

Lasting Change: The Shared Values Process That Makes Companies Great, by Rob Lebow and William L. Simon (Van Nostrand Reinhold, 1997)

A research brief on the Dynamics of Change is available at the Web site of the Principals' Partnership: http://www.principalspartnership.com/library.html

This article focuses on success factors to support change: http://www.butrain.com/business-management-training-courses/ChangeSuccessFactors.asp

This article by Michael Fullan focuses on the principal's role in change: http://www.michaelfullan.ca/Articles_00/11_00.htm

Z

Zooming in on Future Trends

Change is the process by which the future invades our lives.

Alvin Toffler

Think About It

How prepared are you for the future?

Gary Marx of the Educational Research Service suggests that leaders are connected generalists, coming into contact with many people (students, teachers, staff, parents) on many issues (curriculum, instruction, assessment, school activities, school safety, parent involvement). Insightful leaders recognize that things change and change is difficult. Interestingly, Marx suggests that the more difficult issue may be deciding what to work on, rather than the process of change itself. This requires changing old habits and perspectives of the role of the principal.

Six Key Shifts in Perspective

1. Leadership is shifting from a structure that has the leader as a solitary figure at the top of the organization to an increasingly horizontal leadership design. No single person can possibly know everything and the need for multiple conceptions of leadership and pathways to leadership is critical.

2. Access to information is changing the way students learn and teachers teach. The integration of technology as a tool for teaching and learning will only continue to accelerate.

3. Schools are interconnected with all facets of the community and the world. Recognizing the connections with families, community leaders, economic, and political and social systems is essential.

4. The most successful leaders will be those who are able to work with others to create a future. Rather than perpetuating the past they will enthusiastically embrace future trends and use them to shape the future of their school.

5. Educators will continue to struggle with the balance between depth and breadth in the school's program. Leaders must assume the role of looking out for the total system, for balancing the need to deeply understand some things and more narrowly comprehend others. There is a need for both generalists and specialists in any organization.

6. Because life is interconnected and schools are connected to their larger community and the world, learning must occur across disciplines. The focus must be on developing skillful, productive, ethical people who are intellectually curious and engaged in multiple interests across an array of topics.

Responding to Change

As you consider these six shifts, they are connected by one thread: Change will occur. As a principal, you are a change agent (see Chapter A: Achievement is the Focus), but how will you respond to change that which you do not control? Or how can you anticipate change when change is around every corner? There are eight strategies you can use to proactively respond to change.

1. Analyze your environment: Scan the environment in which your school exists—district, community, state, nation, and world. Identify issues that affect your organization and those that affect the

world more broadly. These trends and issues often emerge as important.

2. Monitor changes in the environment: Read voraciously, talk with a broad selection of people in your community, and stay current with trends at the state and national level.

3. Identify the factors needed for success: Look beyond the traditional educational factors (good teachers, money) and consider emerging issues such as the maturing of the community, the ability to acquire and use technology, and the ability to respond to changing conditions.

4. Think about your assumptions: After identifying some of the assumptions you hold about your school and its environment, test those by assessing their degree of certainty (high, medium, low) and the level of impact (high, medium, low). Assumptions play an important role in constructing the future, and they should be as reliable as possible.

5. Develop a vision of an alternative future: Consider the issues you think will have an impact on your school and the factors you identified that are critical to success. Develop a vision of the future that is different from current circumstances. The creation of several alternatives is even better.

6. Consider the alternatives: Discuss each option to identify the most likely and to begin to think about how to respond to this likely situation.

7. Develop plans for needed action: Identify specific steps that can be taken to respond to the anticipated future. "Hedging strategies" can help to cope with undesirable futures. "Shaping strategies" can help create the desired future.

8. Implement plans and monitor progress: Launch initiatives to create the desired future and gather data about progress. Use these data to continue the process by scanning the environment and planning for the future.

These strategies can help you anticipate possible changes for the future and develop manageable transitions to those changes.

Although it is impossible to predict the future, there are several trends that are likely to occur within the next few years. Early in 2008, Ron was asked during a Chicago-area board of education meeting to identify five trends that schools would need to plan for and be prepared to address.

Five Anticipated Trends

1. Increased demands at the state and national levels for greater accountability for improved student learning mean that educators will be pressed to be more successful with all students.
2. Greater access to information about how students learn and research-based strategies for improving student learning will add additional expectations about meeting the individual needs of every learner including those needing the greatest support to those most talented.
3. There will be continued change in the demographics of students in public schools. Schools will be expected to provide a high-quality educational program for groups that have often been underserved by schools.
4. Stable or declining resources will characterize the educational environment. Schools will be expected to be more efficient as well as more effective.
5. An ever-accelerating pace of change in knowledge, research about teaching and learning, and technology will change the way schools are organized and the way teaching and learning occurs. Traditional schools may become obsolete and new learning structures will emerge. Learning will become more integrated rather than separated by content, and multi-age learning environments will become the norm.

How Should I Respond?

Every year we work with dozens of principals, and we've come to appreciate the complexity of their work. Principals are asked to solve some of the most complex and contentious issues in schooling. From these principals we're learned that there are several critical things that principals do:

- Build trust and respect. Skillful leaders recognize that when trust is present, teachers and principals can confront complex and difficult issues. They are able to work together to construct solutions that reflect the school's priorities.

- Stay true to your core values and beliefs. Never compromise your integrity by acting in ways that are contrary to your personal vision. Always work to align your work with the values and beliefs that guide your life.

- Be intellectually curious. Read a lot, think a lot about current and emerging trends. Be open to ways to improve your school even when things are going well.

- Challenge the regularities of schooling. Be comfortable questioning past practice, especially the things that are taken for granted in schools. A good friend of Ron's stated that principals should always be looking for the perfect solution, all the while knowing that no perfect solution exists.

- Build bridges to families and communities. No principal is ever successful without a deep and abiding trust with the families who send their children to your school. Similarly, the community must trust that your values and priorities are focused on students' best interests.

- Hire only the best teachers and other employees. Principals want confidence about the quality of teaching and learning in their school. That means that only the best should ever be hired, and principals should be comfortable deferring a decision until the appropriate candidate is available.

- Cultivate a critical friend, someone outside your school or outside education. Such a friend can provide a fresh perspective on issues you face.

- Enjoy what you do. Relish the impact that principals have on the education of students in their school. But when the enjoyment fades, find ways to reinvigorate your passion or move your career in alternate ways.

A Final Note

Every study of effective schools has found that the most important feature is a highly skilled principal. Principals can have a positive impact on the students in their school, their teachers who work in their building, the families that send their children to the school and the larger school community.

The most effective principals are caring individuals who understand the way a skilled teacher positively impacts the future of their students, who are courageous in tackling complex and contentious issues, and who are confident and steadfast in their vision for a improved learning community.

Skills for Principals

- Develop the capacity for and commitment to high expectations for all students and closing achievement gaps.
- Guide and support professional development that improves teaching and learning to meet the learning needs of every student.
- Create a culture of openness and collaboration.
- Engage teachers and other stakeholders in sharing information, analyzing results, and planning improvement.
- Access varied information sources about trends and issues that may affect education.

If You Would Like More Information . . .

Total Leaders: Applying the Best Future Focused Change Strategies to Education, by Chuck J. Schwahn (American Association of School Administrators, 1998)

Sixteen Trends, Their Profound Impact on Our Future: Implications for Students, Education, Communities, and the Whole of Society, by Gary Marx (Educational Research Service, 2006)

Future-Focused Leadership: Preparing Schools, Students, and Communities for Tomorrow's Realities, by Gary Marx (Association for Supervision and Curriculum Development, 2006)

Five Minds for the Future, by Howard Gardner (Harvard Business School Press, 2007)

"Future Trends Affecting Education," a report from the Education Commission of the States: http://www.ecs.org/clearinghouse/13/27/1327.htm

"Using Data to Create a Successful Future for Our Students," a paper from the Educational Research Service: http//portal.ers.org/content/657/pdf-specwin06a.pdf

"Map of Future Forces Impacting Education," from the Knowledge Works Foundation and the Institute for the Future: http://www.kwfdn.org/map/map.aspx

Future of Education Blog: http://blog.futureofed.org/

Bibliography

Astuto, T. A., Clark, D. L., Read, A., McGree, K., & Fernandez, L. deK. P. (1993). *Challenges to dominant assumptions controlling educational reform.* Andover, MA: Regional Laboratory for the Educational Improvement of the Northeast and Islands.

Beckwith, H. (1997). *Selling the invisible: A field guide to modern marketing.* New York: Warner Books.

Beckwith, H., & Beckwith, C. C. (2007). *You, Inc.: The art of selling yourself.* New York: Warner Business Books.

Bennis, W., & Goldsmith, J. (2003). *Learning to lead: A workbook on becoming a leader* (3rd ed.). New York: Basic Books.

Bernhardt, V. L. (1998). *Data analysis for comprehensive schoolwide improvement.* Larchmont, NY: Eye On Education.

Bernhardt, V. L. (2003). *Using data to improve student learning.* Larchmont, NY: Eye On Education.

Black, P., Harrison, C., Lee, C., Marshall, B., & William, D. (2004). Working inside the black box: Assessment for learning in the classroom. *Phi Delta Kappan, 86*(1), 9–21.

Blackburn, B. R. (2005). *Classroom motivation from A to Z: How to engage your students in learning.* Larchmont, NY: Eye On Education.

Blackburn, B. R. (2007). *Classroom instruction from A to Z: How to promote student learning.* Larchmont, NY: Eye On Education.

Blackburn, B. R. (2008). *Literacy from A to Z: Engaging students in reading, writing, speaking, and listening.* Larchmont, NY: Eye On Education

Blackburn, B. R. (2008). *Rigor is not a four-letter word.* Larchmont, NY: Eye On Education.

Blanchard, K. (2007). *Leading at a higher level: Blanchard on leadership and creating high performing organizations.* Upper Saddle River, NJ: Prentice Hall.

Blink, R. J. (2007). *Data-driven instructional leadership.* Larchmont, NY: Eye On Education.

Bolman, L. G., & Deal, T. E. (1995). *Leading with soul: An uncommon journey of spirit.* San Francisco: Jossey-Bass.

Bolman, L. G., & Deal, T. E. (2008). *Reframing organizations: Artistry, choice, and leadership* (4th ed.). San Francisco: Jossey-Bass.

Breaux, A. L. (2003). *101 "Answers" for new teachers and their mentors: Effective teaching tips for daily classroom use.* Larchmont, NY: Eye On Education.

Buck, F. (2008). *Get organized! Time management for school leaders.* Larchmont, NY: Eye On Education.

Cambron-McCabe, N. H., McCarthy, M., & Tomas, S. (2009). *Legal rights of teachers and students* (2nd ed.). Boston: Allyn & Bacon.

Canady, R. L., & Rettig, M. D. (2008). *Elementary school scheduling: Enhancing instruction for student achievement.* Larchmont, NY: Eye On Education.

Clarridge, P. B., & Whitaker, E. M. (1997). *Rolling the elephant over: How to effect large-scale change in the reporting process.* Portsmouth, NH: Heinemann.

Cogan, M. L. (1973). *Clinical supervision.* Boston: Houghton Mifflin.

Collins, J. (2001). *Good to great: Why some companies make the leap—and others don't.* New York: HarperBusiness.

Constantino, S. M. (2003). *Making your school family friendly.* Reston, VA: National Association of Secondary School Principals.

Cooke, G. J. (2007). *Keys to success for urban principals* (2nd ed.). Thousand Oaks, CA: Corwin.

Covey, S. R. (1991). *Principle-centered leadership.* New York: Summit Books.

Covey, S. R. (2004). *The 8th habit: From effectiveness to greatness.* New York: Free Press.

Danielson, C. (2002). *Enhancing student achievement: A framework for school improvement.* Alexandria, VA: Association for Supervision and Curriculum Development.

Danielson, C. (2007). *Enhancing professional practice: A framework for teaching* (2nd ed.). Alexandria, VA: Association for Supervision and Curriculum Development.

Danielson, C., & McGreal, T. L. (2000). *Teacher evaluation to enhance professional practice.* Alexandria, VA: Association for Supervision and Curriculum Development.

Darling-Hammond, L (1997). *The right to learn: A blueprint for creating schools that work.* San Francisco: Jossey-Bass.

Deal, T. E., & Peterson, K. D. (1999). *Shaping school culture: The heart of leadership.* San Francisco: Jossey-Bass.

Deal, T. E., & Peterson, K. D. (2009). *Shaping school culture: Pitfalls, paradoxes and promises* (2nd ed.). San Francisco: Jossey-Bass.

De Pree, M. (1989). *Leadership is an art.* New York: Doubleday.

Downey, C. J., Steffy, B. E., English, F. W., Frase, L. E., & Poston, W. K. (2004). *The three-minute classroom walk-through: Changing school supervisory practice one teacher at a time.* Thousand Oaks, CA: Corwin.

DuFour, R., & Eaker, R. (1998). *Professional learning communities at work: Best practices for enhancing student achievement.* Bloomington, IN: National Educational Service.

DuFour, R., DuFour, R., Eaker, R., & Many, T. (2006). *Learning by doing: A handbook for professional learning communities at work.* Bloomington, IN: Solution Tree.

Eaker, R., DuFour, R., & DuFour, R. (2002). *Getting started: Reculturing schools to become professional learning communities.* Bloomington, IN: Solution Tree.

Epstein, J. L. (2001). *School, family, and community partnerships: Preparing educators and improving schools.* Boulder, CO: Westview Press.

Fink, E., & Resnick, L. B. (2001). *Developing principals as instructional leaders.* Pittsburgh, PA: University of Pittsburgh, Learning Research and Development Center.

Fleck, F. (2005). *What successful principals do! 169 tips for principals.* Larchmont, NY: Eye On Education.

Friedman, T. L. (2005). *The world is flat: A brief history of the twenty-first century.* New York: Farrar, Straus and Giroux.

Friedman, T. L. (2008). *Hot, flat, and crowded: Why we need a green revolution and how it can renew America.* New York; Farrar, Straus and Giroux.

Fullan, M. (1993). *Change forces: Probing the depths of educational reform.* Bristol, PA: Falmer Press.

Fullan, M. (2001). *Leading in a culture of change.* San Francisco: Jossey-Bass.

Fullan, M. (2005). *Leadership and sustainability: Systems thinkers in action.* Thousand Oaks, CA: Corwin.

Fullan, M. (2007). *The new meaning of educational change* (4th ed.). New York: Teachers College Press.

Gardner, H. (2007). *Five minds for the future.* Boston: Harvard Business School Press.

Garmston, R., & Wellman, B. (1999). *The adaptive school: A sourcebook for developing collaborative groups.* Norwood, MA: Christopher-Gordon.

Gladwell, M. (2002). *The tipping point: How little things can make a big difference.* Boston: Little, Brown.

Glickman, C. D., Gordon, S. P., & Ross-Gordon, J. M. (2004). *Supervision and instructional leadership: A developmental approach* (6th ed.). Boston: Allyn & Bacon.

Godin, S. (2001). *Unleashing the ideavirus.* New York: Hyperion.

Goldberg, S. J. (2008). Questions replace feedback. *Principal Leadership, 8*(8), 64–66.

Goldhammer, R. (1969). *Clinical supervision: Special methods for the supervision of teachers.* New York: Holt, Rinehart and Winston.

Gray, S. P., & Streshly, W. A. (2008). *From good schools to great schools: What their principals do well.* Thousand Oaks, CA: Corwin Press.

Guskey, T. R., & Bailey, J. M. (2001). *Developing grading and reporting systems for student learning.* Thousand Oaks, CA: Corwin.

Hall, G. E., & Hord, S. M. (2001). *Implementing change: Patterns, principles, and potholes.* Boston: Allyn & Bacon.

Hill, J. D., & Flynn, K. M. (2006). *Classroom instruction that works with English language learners.* Alexandria, VA: Association for Supervision and Curriculum Development.

Hord, S. M. (1997). *Professional learning communities: Communities of continuous inquiry and improvement.* Austin, TX: Southwest Educational Development Laboratory.

Hoy, A. W., & Hoy, W. K. (2003). *Instructional leadership: A learning-centered guide.* Boston: Allyn & Bacon.

Hoy, W. K., & Tarter, C. J. (2008). *Administrators solving the problems of practice: Decision-making concepts, cases, and consequences* (3rd ed.). Boston: Pearson Education.

Hunter, M. (1982). *Mastery teaching.* Thousand Oaks, CA: Corwin.

Kanter, R. M. (1983). *The change masters: Innovations for productivity in the American corporation.* New York: Simon & Schuster.

Kouzes, J. M., & Posner, B. Z. (2003). *Credibility: How leaders gain and lose it, why people demand it* (2nd ed.). San Francisco: Jossey-Bass.

Kush, C. (2000). *Cybercitizen: How to use your computer to fight for all the issues you care about.* New York: St. Martin's Griffin.

Kush, C. (2001). *Grassroots games: Preparing your advocates for the political arena.* Washington, DC: American Society of Association Executives.

Kush, C. (2004). *The one-hour activist: The 15 most powerful actions you can take to fight for the issues and candidates you care about.* San Francisco: Jossey-Bass.

Lambert, L. (1998). *Building leadership capacity in schools.* Alexandria, VA: Association for Supervision and Curriculum Development.

Lambert, L. (2003). *Leadership capacity for lasting school improvement.* Alexandria, VA: Association for Supervision and Curriculum Development.

Lambert, L., Walker, D., Zimmerman, D. P., Cooper, J. E., Lambert, M. D., Gardner, M. E., & Szabo, M. (2002). *The constructivist leader.* New York: Teachers College Press.

Langer, G. M., Colton, A. B., & Goff, L. S. (2003). *Collaborative analysis of student work: Improving teaching and learning.* Alexandria, VA: Association for Supervision and Curriculum Development.

Little, J. W., & McLaughlin, M. W. (1993). *Teachers' work: Individuals, colleagues, and contexts.* New York: Teachers College Press.

Marzano, R. J. (2000). *Transforming classroom grading.* Alexandria, VA: Association for Supervision and Curriculum Development.

Marzano, R. J. (2003). *Classroom management that works.* Alexandria, VA: Association for Supervision and Curriculum Development.

Marzano, R. J. (2003). *What works in schools: Translating research into action.* Alexandria, VA: Association for Supervision and Curriculum Development.

Marzano, R. J., Pickering, D. J., & Pollock, J. E. (2001). *Classroom instruction that works: Research-based strategies for increasing student achievement.* Alexandria, VA: Association for Supervision and Curriculum Development.

Marzano, R. J., Waters, T., & McNulty, B. A. (2005). *School leadership that works: From research to results.* Alexandria, VA: Association for Supervision and Curriculum Development.

Marx, G. (2006). *Future-focused leadership: Preparing schools, students, and communities for tomorrow's realities.* Alexandria, VA: Association for Supervision and Curriculum Development.

Marx, G. (2006). *Sixteen trends, their profound impact on our future: Implications for students, education, communities, and the whole of society.* Alexandria, VA: Educational Research Service.

Maslow, A. H. (1968). *Toward a psychology of being.* New York: John Wiley.

Maxwell, J. C. (1999). *The 21 indispensable qualities of a leader: Becoming the person that people will want to follow.* Nashville, TN: Thomas Nelson.

McLaughlin, M. W., Talbert, J. E., & Bascia, N. (1993). *The contexts of teaching in secondary schools: Teachers' realities.* New York: Teachers College Press.

O'Rourke, A., Provenzano, J., Bellamy, T., & Ballek, K. (2007). *Countdown to the principalship: A resource guide for beginning principals.* Larchmont, NY: Eye On Education.

Peterson, K. D., & Deal, T. E. (2002). *The shaping school culture fieldbook.* San Francisco: Jossey-Bass.

Popham, W. J. (2008). *Transformative assessment.* Alexandria, VA: Association for Supervision and Curriculum Development.

Reeves, D. B. (2006). *The learning leader: How to focus school improvement for better results.* Alexandria, VA: Association for Supervision and Curriculum Development.

Rosen, E. (2000). *The anatomy of buzz: How to create word-of-mouth marketing.* New York: Doubleday/Currency.

Rosenholtz, S. J. (1989). *Teachers' workplace: The social organization of schools.* New York: Longman

Rothstein-Fisch, C., & Trumbull, E. (2008). *Managing diverse classrooms: How to build on students' cultural strengths.* Alexandria, VA: Association for Supervision and Curriculum Development.

Schlechty, P. C. (2001). *Shaking up the schoolhouse: How to support and sustain educational innovation.* San Francisco: Jossey-Bass.

Schmoker, M. (1999). *Results: The key to continuous school improvement* (2nd ed.). Alexandria, VA; Association for Supervision and Curriculum Development.

Schmoker, M. (2006). *Results now: How we can achieve unprecedented improvements in teaching and learning.* Alexandria, VA: Association for Supervision and Curriculum Development.

Senge, P. M. (2006). *The fifth discipline: The art and practice of the learning organization.* New York: Doubleday.

Sergiovanni, T. J. (1996). *Leadership for the schoolhouse: How is it different? Why is it important?* San Francisco: Jossey-Bass.

Shapiro, J. P., & Stefkovich, J. A. (2005). *Ethical leadership and decision making in education: Applying theoretical perspectives to complex dilemmas.* Mahwah, NJ: Lawrence Erlbaum.

Silberman, M. (1999). *101 ways to make meetings active: Surefire ideas to engage your group.* San Francisco: Jossey-Bass.

Singleton, G. E., & Linton, C. (2006). *Courageous conversations about race: A field guide for achieving equity in schools.* Thousand Oaks, CA: Corwin.

Sizer, T. R. (1992). *Horace's compromise: The dilemma of the American high school.* Boston: Houghton Mifflin.

Sullivan, S., & Glanz, J. (2005). *Supervision that improves teaching: Strategies and techniques* (2nd ed.). Thousand Oaks, CA: Corwin.

Tate, J. S., & Dunklee, D. R. (2005). *Strategic listening for school leaders.* Thousand Oaks, CA: Corwin.

Thernstrom, A., & Thernstrom, S. (2003). *No excuses: Closing the racial gap in learning.* New York: Simon & Schuster.

Tichy, N. M., & Bennis, W. G. (2007). *Judgment: How winning leaders make great calls.* New York: Penguin.

Ubben, G. C., Hughes, L. W., & Norris, C. J. (2006). *The principal: Creative leadership for excellence in schools* (6th ed.). Boston: Allyn & Bacon.

Wahlstrom, D. (1999). *Using data to improve student achievement.* Suffolk, VA: Successline.

Wellman, B., & Lipton, L. (2004). *Data-driven dialogue: A facilitator's guide to collaborative inquiry.* Sherman, CT: MiraVia.

Whitaker, T. (2002). *What great principals do differently: Fifteen things that matter most.* Larchmont, NY: Eye On Education.

Whitaker, T., & Fiore, D. J. (2001). *Dealing with difficult parents (and with parents in difficult situations).* Larchmont, NY: Eye On Education.

Williams, B. (2003). *Closing the achievement gap: A vision for changing beliefs and practices* (2nd ed.). Alexandria, VA: Association for Supervision and Curriculum Development.

Williamson, R. (2009). *Scheduling to improve student learning.* Westerville, OH: National Middle School Association.

Zepeda, S. J. (2007). *Instructional supervision: Applying tools and concepts.* Larchmont, NY: Eye On Education.

Appendix I

Educational Leadership Policy Standards: ISLLC 2008

Educational Leadership
Policy Standards: ISLLC 2008

Adopted by the National Policy Board for Educational Administration, December 2007

Standard 1

An education leader promotes the success of every student by facilitating the development, articulation, implementation, and stewardship of a vision of learning that is shared and supported by all stakeholders.

Functions		Chapters
a.	Collaboratively develop and implement a shared vision and mission	O, V, W
b.	Collect and use data to identify goals, assess organizational effectiveness, and promote organizational learning	D, Y
c.	Create and implement plans to achieve goals	N, V, W, Y
d.	Promote continuous and sustainable improvement	V, W, Y
e.	Monitor and evaluate progress and revise plans	D, W

Standard 2

An education leader promotes the success of every student by advocating, nurturing and sustaining a school culture and instructional program conducive to student learning and staff professional growth.

Functions		Chapters
a.	Nurture and sustain a culture of collaboration, trust, learning, and high expectations	A, B, I, N
b.	Create a comprehensive, rigorous, and coherent curricular program	G, I

Functions	Chapters
c. Create a personalized and motivating learning environment for students	I
d. Supervise instruction	I, Q, S
e. Develop assessment and accountability systems to monitor student progress	G, L
f. Develop the instructional and leadership capacity of staff	L, P
g. Maximize time spent on quality instruction	I, J, M
h. Promote the use of the most effective and appropriate technologies to support teaching and learning	I, L, X
i. Monitor and evaluate the impact of the instructional program	D, Q

Standard 3

An education leader promotes the success of every student by ensuring management of the organization, operation, and resources for a safe, efficient, and effective learning environment.

Functions	Chapters
a. Monitor and evaluate the management and operational systems	D, U
b. Obtain, allocate, align, and efficiently utilize human, fiscal, and technological resources	F, J, M, Q
c. Promote and protect the welfare and safety of student and staff	E, U
d. Develop the capacity for distributed leadership	N, O, W
e. Ensure teacher and organizational time is focused to support quality instruction and student learning	C, J

Standard 4

An education leader promotes the success of every student by collaborating with faculty and community members, responding to diverse community interests and needs, and mobilizing community resources.

Functions		Chapters
a.	Collect and analyze data and information pertinent to the educational environment	D, Z
b.	Promote understanding, appreciation, and use of the community's diverse cultural, social, and intellectual resources	T
c.	Build and sustain positive relationships with families and caregivers	B, K, T
d.	Build and sustain productive relationships with community partners	K, T

Standard 5

An education leader promotes the success of every student by acting with integrity, fairness, and in an ethical manner.

Functions		Chapters
a.	Ensure a system of accountability for every student's academic and social success	E, Q
b.	Model principles of self-awareness, reflective practice, transparency, and ethical behavior	V
c.	Safeguard the values of democracy, equity, and diversity	R, X
d.	Consider and evaluate the potential moral and legal consequences of decision making	R, V
e.	Promote social justice and ensure that individual student needs inform all aspects of schooling	E, X

Standard 6

An education leader promotes the success of every student by understanding, responding to, and influencing the political, social, economic, legal, and cultural context.

Functions		Chapters
a.	Advocate for children, families, and caregivers	T, X
b.	Act to influence local, district, state, and national decisions affecting student learning	Z
c.	Assess, analyze, and anticipate emerging trends and initiatives in order to adapt leadership strategies	Z

Appendix II

Standards for Advanced Programs in Educational Leadership, Educational Leadership Constituent Council

Standards for Advanced Programs in Educational Leadership, Educational Leadership Constituent Council

Published by National Policy Board for Educational Administration, January, 2002

Standard 1.0

Candidates who complete the program are educational leaders who have the knowledge and ability to promote the success of all students by facilitating the development, articulation, implementation, and stewardship of a school or district vision of learning supported by the school community.

	Chapters
1.1 Develop a vision	D, O, V, W
1.2 Articulate a vision	A, N, V
1.3 Implement a vision	N, V, W, Y
1.4 Steward a vision	A, V
1.5 Promote community involvement in the vision	O, V

Standard 2.0

Candidates who complete the program are educational leaders who have the knowledge and ability to promote the success of all students by promoting a positive school culture, providing an effective instructional program, applying best practice to student learning, and designing comprehensive professional growth plans for staff.

	Chapters
2.1 Promote positive school culture	B, N, W
2.2 Provide effective instructional program	D, I, L, Q, S
2.3 Apply best practice to student learning	G, I, L, Q
2.4 Design comprehensive professional growth plans	P

Standard 3.0

Candidates who complete the program are educational leaders who have the knowledge and ability to promote the success of all students by managing the organization, operations, and resources in a way that promotes a safe, efficient, and effective learning environment.

	Chapters
3.1 Manage the organization	C, J
3.2 Manage operations	E, M, U
3.3 Manage resources	F, Q

Standard 4.0

Candidates who complete the program are educational leaders who have the knowledge and ability to promote the success of all students by collaborating with families and other community members, responding to diverse community interests and needs, and mobilizing community resources.

	Chapters
4.1 Collaborate with families and other community members	T
4.2 Respond to community interests and needs	K, T
4.3 Mobilize community resources	K, T

Standard 5.0

Candidates who complete the program are educational leaders who have the knowledge and ability to promote the success of all students by acting with integrity, fairly, and in an ethical manner.

	Chapters
5.1 Acts with integrity	R, V
5.2 Acts fairly	E, V
5.3 Acts ethically	R, V, X

Standard 6.0

Candidates who complete the program are educational leaders who have the knowledge and ability to promote the success of all students by understanding, responding to, and influencing the larger political, social, economic, legal, and cultural context.

	Chapters
6.1 Understand the larger context	H, Z
6.2 Respond to the larger context	Z
6.3 Influence the larger context	Z

Standard 7.0

The internship provides significant opportunities for candidates to synthesize and apply the knowledge and practice and develop the skills identified in Standards 1-6 through substantial, sustained, standards-based work in real settings, planned and guided by the institution and school district personnel for graduate credit.

	Chapters
7.1 Substantial	Not Applicable
7.2 Sustained	
7.3 Standards-based	
7.4 Real settings	
7.5 Planned and guided cooperatively	
7.6 Credit	